One Life, Three Countries

Otto Gaczol
with Andrew Gaczol

One Life, Three Countries
The story of a 'New Australian'

One Life, Three Countries: The story of a 'New Australian'
ISBN 978 1 76041
Copyright © Otto Gaczol and Andrew Gaczol 2020
Photo credits –
Cover image: background immigration document provided by and with
the permission of the National Archives of Australia
p. 50: map courtesy of The Department of History,
United States Military Academy at West Point
p. 87: images of the Personalausweis with permission of
the Bielefeld Einwohnermeldeamt
p. 97: MS *Seven Seas*, 1953–1977. Canadian Museum of Immigration
at Pier 21 (DI2013.534.1)
p. 117: Ellis/Elsasser family courtesy of the Dunstan family

First published 2015
This expanded edition published 2020

GINNINDERRA PRESS
PO Box 3461 Port Adelaide 5015
www.ginninderrapress.com.au

Contents

Introduction		7
One	Beginnings and Bielitz	9
Two	Occupied Poland	19
Three	Flight from the Red Army	41
Four	Post-war Germany	65
Five	Decision to Travel	91
Six	Arrival in Australia	104
Epilogue		124
Bibliography		126
Notes		138

Introduction

With the 70th anniversary of the end of World War II, the last of the generation who lived through it are slowly departing the stage. As we know, the consequences of that war in Europe were enormous. Poland suffered terribly, Germany was devastated, defeated and divided, and millions of people throughout the continent were either dead or permanently uprooted from their homelands.

Australia, too, felt the effects of that conflict. The war between the western Allies and Japan in the Pacific had exposed the nation's isolation and vulnerability when the assumed promise of protection from the British empire proved to be illusory. The threatened Japanese onslaught on Australia spawned the post-war policy of 'populate or perish' and Australia opened itself to large-scale non-British immigration for the first time since federation, partly to stimulate the economy but mostly out of a sense of national survival.

My father's life was shaped by these profound events. As an ethnic German boy who grew-up in pre-war Poland, he lived through the Nazi occupation just 30 kilometres away from Auschwitz and then, in January 1945, fled west as a 14-year-old refugee when the Soviet Union's Red Army turned the tide against the Wehrmacht and made its way to Berlin. As a young adult, he took advantage of Australia's large-scale post-war immigration program to come here for what he thought was a two-year adventure. It ended up being much longer than that.

Most stories have been told and retold, and a certain predictable and socially acceptable lore has developed on this, the world's most destructive conflict. The story of the Germans, their uprooting and suffering through their flight and forced expulsion during the final days of the war and the period immediately after, is not one that gets much coverage or interest due to the responsibility of Nazi Germany for initiating the war. Nonetheless, these events are real and perhaps with the passing of time they can now be told with greater frequency and garner greater interest, though not without forgetting their original context.

My father's story is, then, just one of millions of similar stories from people from that generation who lived through those extraordinary times. It is a remarkable story that serves to remind us of that period of great suffering and upheaval that occurred only one human lifetime ago. His journey through pre-war and occupied Poland, post-war Germany and then eventually to Australia tells a story difficult for those of us who grew up in an era of peace and prosperity to comprehend. Listening to these stories as a child, they do not resonate much until, as an adult, one is confronted with one's own life choices of relocating to a different city or living overseas. Suddenly, one then appreciates how remarkable those stories are, especially as they occurred before the era of easy international travel and instant global communications.

As mentioned, although part of this book touches on historically sensitive events – such as the post-war expulsion of the Germans and the carpet bombing by the western Allies of German cities – it is important to note that the book's intent is to tell one person's story and not to advocate a political cause. In telling this story, and touching on those controversial events, I in no way excuse the atrocities of the Nazis or minimise the genocides committed against the European Jews and other ethnic groups by that regime. I strongly reject any revisionist, anti-Semitic or pro-Nazi perspectives. Hitler and the Nazi regime brought nothing but death and suffering to the peoples of Europe, and destruction and shame to Germany and the German people. The reader should also note that, during the Nazi period, my father was a child and as an adult he too fully acknowledges the regime's criminal nature.

Although I have done the background research and the writing itself, the story is my father's and it is written in his voice.

Andrew Gaczol
Canberra, 2015

One

Beginnings and Bielitz

Perhaps the worst place to have been born in the first half of the 20th century was central Europe. The tides of armies and history that swept over the European plain caused untold suffering and upheaval during the 20th century. But it was here where I and my family were born and it has, without question, shaped our history.

Born in the first decade of the 20th century, both my parents were citizens of the then Austria-Hungary empire. Although technically a single nation-state, Austria-Hungary was a country with many nationalities and ethnic groups. The two largest ethnic groups were Germans and Hungarians. There were also Poles, Croats, Bosnians, Serbians, Italians, Czechs, Ruthenes, Slovenes, Slovaks and Romanians; in total, some 15 different languages were spoken in the empire.[1]

My family reflected this ethnic mix. My mother, Maria Hrbacek, was born in Vienna in 1907, while my father, Thaddeus Gaczol, was born in late 1906 in Zakopane in the north-eastern region of the empire called Galicia.

Although they were both Austrians, my father almost certainly saw himself as Polish and in the short time that he and my mother lived together as a married couple my schooling was at the local Polish school, partly because he preferred it but also because, as a small business owner and Polish citizen, he was obliged to send me there. He was not, however, anti-German and was happy to have us speak in German at home even though he could speak only Polish himself.

My mother, on the other hand, had a Czech family name, spoke German, Polish and Czech and, although she considered herself Austrian, had no reservations in signing up to the *Deutsche Volksliste* (German people's list) during World War II, through which she acquired German citizenship. Austria had, in 1938, already been annexed by Nazi Germany. Today, Zakopane is a picturesque skiing resort in Poland near the border with Slovakia, while Vienna is, of course, the beautiful and magnificent capital of modern Austria.

I was born in the second half of 1930 in Bielsko-Biala (Bielitz in German) in Upper Silesia (Oberschlesien). The family story is a little confusing and has been pieced together through fragments of memory and family conversations.

My own mother was born out of wedlock and was taken in by her mother's sister – my great aunt, Antonina Metka – who couldn't have children of her own. Although she was at one stage married to a Danube river boat captain, they divorced due to his alcoholism and Antonina ended up living unmarried with a man whom I called Uncle Erich. Antonina was a professional chef and Uncle Erich was also a chef and a baker who eventually built up a successful bakery business in Bielsko-Biala.

My mother received her education, both school and high school, through a monastery in Bielsko-Biala. At 16 years of age, she returned to Vienna with Uncle Erich's sister, Auntie Greta, through whom she learnt office work, such as typing and shorthand.

I don't know how my father ended up in Bielsko-Biala, but he was Uncle Erich's apprentice, and it was through Uncle Erich's business that he learnt to be a pastry chef; presumably that is how he and my mother met. My mother and father were married in May 1930. The fact that I was born less than nine months later may explain my parents' relationship.

Upper Silesia

Upper Silesia itself, in a sense, reflects the mixed ethnic make-up of my own family. Part of imperial Germany's frontier with Austria-Hungary and Russia before World War I, its status was strongly disputed following that war, with both the democratic Weimar Germany and the newly independent state of Poland claiming the region as their own. Economically, it was quite a prize, given its coal mining, zinc mining and other industries. The Upper Silesian industrial triangle was second only to the Ruhr valley as an industrial region in imperial Germany, and in 1913

Upper Silesian coal-fields accounted for 21 per cent of all German coal production.[2]

The dispute was of such importance that its resolution was a clause in the Versailles Treaty of 1919 and ultimately involved the deployment of French and British troops, three Polish uprisings during 1919–1921, and a plebiscite. Although the plebiscite resulted in 706,000 votes for the region to remain part of Germany and 479,000 votes to become part of Poland, the region was eventually divided, with the south-eastern part being incorporated into Poland.[3] This south-eastern region, although geographically relatively small, held three-quarters of Silesia's coal production and nearly two-thirds of its steelworks.[4]

The division of inter-war Upper Silesia into separate German and Polish ethnic camps does not in itself fully explain the clash of identity that existed, and still exists, in this part of central Europe. The vast majority of Polish-speaking Upper Silesians served loyally in the imperial German army during World War I,[5] and voting patterns in the plebiscite and other elections did not necessarily follow linguistic or ethnic lines.[6] It is not unusual in ethnic borderlands, such as Upper Silesia, for many people to show an indifference to ethno-linguistic nationalism, as these issues normally take second place to everyday life.[7] There is also an Upper Silesian identity separate and yet combined with the German and Polish communities which still manifests itself within the region.[8] This identity also partly explains why after World War II, Upper Silesia, with its mixed-language, bilingual, Catholic population, largely avoided the expulsions that occurred in other areas where the borders were altered – indeed, over 750,000 Upper Silesians remained in their homes after World War II; up to 90 per cent in some rural areas were spared expulsion.[9] After World War II, there remained a significant ethnic German community in Upper Silesia.

Miroslav Klose, Germany's record-breaking football player – whose father Josef was an ethnically German Silesian – was born in Opole (Oppeln) in Upper Silesia in 1978 and he and his family eventually moved to the Federal Republic of Germany. Another current German football player, Lukas Podolski, is also of Upper Silesian heritage, having been born in Gliwice (Gleiwitz) near Katowice (Kattowitz).

My home town: Bielsko-Biala

Having been created on 1 January 1951, Bielsko-Biala is today a united city with a population of about 180,000. However, in the 1930s it consisted of two separate cities of Bielsko and Biala, separated by the Biala (Bialka in German) River. Bielsko, which for centuries belonged to the Duchy of Cieszyn, was founded in 1312. In 1723, on the opposite bank of the river, the city of Biala came into being. In 1772, Biala was annexed by Austria and included in the crown land of Galicia. In 1918, both cities became part of the new Polish state, though a significant part of the population was ethnic German.[10] It was then, and remains today, an attractive city with both its town hall and main post office being built in an impressive late 19th century architectural style and it is occasionally referred to as 'Little Vienna' for this reason.

My own observations as a child growing up in the 1930s were that the

Town Hall, Bielsko-Biala. (Andrew Gaczol)

separate German and Polish communities didn't necessarily mix much but the relationship overall was benign – at least until the six months or so before the outbreak of World War II. The apartment building where we lived had both Polish and German/Austrian families and my childhood friends included both Polish and German friends. We spent a good deal of time playing together as children do. There was also the usual childish teasing and fighting which involved ethnic insults such as 'Polaks' and 'you bloody Germans', but it didn't last long and we went back to being friends again soon after.

Bielsko-Biala's Jewish community

There was, of course, also a Jewish community in Bielsko-Biala, one that ultimately went back many centuries. The first mention of Jews in Bielsko comes from 1653; and two complaints about Jewish tax collectors were

Roman Catholic Church of the Providence of God, just around the corner from my home on Tuchmacherstrasse. (Andrew Gaczol)

recorded in 1677. Jews in Bielsko strove to establish an independent community from the beginning of the 19th century, but until 1865 they were formally part of the community of Cieszyn. A synagogue was built in the late 1830s with a cemetery and religious school established in the late 1840s. Over the course of the 19th century, the Jews of Bielsko became strongly 'Germanised'; that is, they spoke German and saw themselves as Germans.[11] An outstanding scholar, Sha'ul Horowitz, was the rabbi in Bielsko from 1888 to 1896 and another famous Jew from Bielsko was Michael Berkowicz, who was Theodor Herzl's Hebrew secretary.[12]

In 1869, the Jewish community had totalled 1,102 people but by 1930 it had risen to 4,430. In the 1920s and 1930s, Bielsko was an important centre of Zionism and also of pro-German integration and for the entire interwar period the community was torn between these two positions. The press developed initially in German and from the mid-1930s in Polish as well.[13] I remember quite well seeing them around town. While there were secular Jews, there were also many Orthodox Jews who stood out quite clearly because of their distinctive black outfits, curly beards, kippa skullcaps and large furry hats. Like the interactions between the German and Polish communities, they kept mostly to themselves but had amicable enough relationships with both communities from what I could see. My mother and Antonina saw Jewish shop owners as friendly, polite and willing – unlike others – to provide credit to their customers. Given the times and the place, there was, however, a degree of anti-Semitism present in both communities, mostly driven by jealously about the Jewish community's perceived wealth. The 1930s were, of course, the time of the Great Depression and there was resentment at those who had wealth during those very tough times, and every Jew was thought of as being rich. I myself must confess an incident when I was about five years old. My friends and I went along to the Jewish quarter to try to smash the windows of the synagogue by throwing stones. It was surrounded by a seven-or-eight-foot-high iron fence and as small children we couldn't throw anywhere near far enough to do any damage. In fact, my coat pockets were so full of stones I could barely move. It must be said that my friends and I were children and far too young to understand anti-Semitism and this event should certainly be viewed as childhood high jinks rather than anything political.

More seriously, though, was an event from that same time that has stayed in my memory. My recollection is that there was an incident where a Pole had supposedly been killed by a Jew, but the facts were hard to establish. Some in the Polish community responded with revenge beatings on the city's Jewish residents and the Polish police were conspicuously slow to respond. Also, graffiti was painted on Jewish shops and Jewish-owned buildings saying 'Don't shop at Jewish shops.' Strangely, a few days later, someone scratched out the word 'Don't' on all the graffiti leaving the message as 'shop at Jewish shops' in an almost comic parody of the original message. This edited graffiti remained on the walls for quite some time.

The Great Depression: hard times for our family

The mid-1930s were also a difficult time for our family. My mother had inherited Uncle Erich's bakery after he died in 1932 from stomach cancer but my father, who ran the bakery, went broke partly because of the economic slowdown of the Great Depression but also partly because he lent money which was never repaid. He lost the family bakery business and despite the birth of their second child – my sister Irene – my mother kicked my father out and they separated in mid-1935. Along with Antonina, my sister and I stayed with our mother, but a single mother, and elderly aunt and two children, was not an appealing proposition to many landlords. Our family found it difficult to find an apartment and we ended up moving house a number of times. This experience would eventually play a role in my decision to remain in Australia when I had my own family.

My mother also withdrew me from the Polish school and had my education continue at a German kindergarten. It was quite a different experience at the German schools. My Polish school was run by nuns. Although they certainly punished you if you did something wrong, the school was a little chaotic. The German school was much better disciplined and organised and we were even required to wear uniforms with a blue dustcoat. Despite it being a German school, we were also taught to write and speak Polish and it did not teach any political propaganda.

I don't have many memories of my father at that time. Apart from when he came over once a week to pay alimony, we saw him once every six months or so. He was a keen bicycle rider and had a number of bikes. It sounds strange today, but at that time in Poland bicycles had to be registered just as cars do today. I distinctly remember the little number plates that hung directly under the seat. As he was broke, my father couldn't pay the registration and he lost the bikes when they were confiscated by the taxation department. His other passion was German shepherd dogs, and he had three of them as well. Two of them were killed after having been run over by cars. This wasn't too surprising as dogs, and indeed people, weren't used to seeing cars around, as they were very much only for those who could afford them. Although today cars are everywhere, in the mid-1930s there were few to be seen and as a pedestrian you might see a car around town once an hour or so.

My father and I, with one of his dogs, Bielsko-Biala, 1934. (Otto Gaczol)

The march towards war

The serious tensions that developed between the Polish and German communities began six months before the start of World War II. In violation of the September 1938 Munich Agreement, Nazi Germany occupied Czechoslovakia in March 1939.[14] Almost immediately afterwards, the Nazi regime began to make territorial demands on Poland for the return to the German Reich of Danzig – then a League of Nations free city – and the Pomorcze (Posen) region: the 'Polish corridor'. In April, the British and French signed a mutual assistance pact with the Polish government, promising to come to Poland's military aid should Poland be attacked. By August, plans had been finalised between the Nazi regime in Germany and the Soviet Union under Stalin to invade Poland and partition it once more.[15]

The situation grew more intense as the outbreak of war drew closer. My mother was on the receiving end of an outburst by a Polish soldier for having bought German magazines. He was quite severe on her, even though he eventually walked away and nothing came of it. More seriously, I remember that one of our neighbours who lived in the building across the street was apparently a Polish nationalist who belonged to a group of agitators who called themselves, if I remember correctly, the Underground Fighters. The 13-year-old boy of the family, the son of the nationalist, would regularly come to our home and taunt my mother on behalf of his father. As tensions increased politically between Nazi Germany and Poland during 1939, the taunting increased from 'What are you doing here – why don't you go back to Germany?' to the point where death threats were being made. These included my mother being asked, 'My father would like to know how you would like to die – hanged or shot?' Eventually my mother got fed up and lost her temper at the boy, telling him to go back to his father and challenging him to come and make these threats himself rather than be a coward and send his young son. Three days before the war broke out, I saw him and his family leaving Bielsko-Biala in the direction of Krakow. We never saw him again, but about two weeks later the rest of the family returned without him to their flat in their building. But they didn't stay long and eventually left permanently.

In those final months before the war, I also got teased and taunted with anti-German insults by boys who I thought were Polish but who eventually presented themselves as Germans once the war had broken out and Poland was occupied. Some of them even ended up joining the Hitler Youth. Perhaps, like me, they were of a mixed German/Polish family and just saw me as a target for some 'fun', or they were trying to cover up their own nationality.

Just a few weeks before war's outbreak, Antonina left Poland. She still held an Austrian passport and, given that Austria was now a province of an expanded Nazi Germany, she and some of the other Germans left the city for fear of internment. State propaganda was also ramped up by both sides as September approached. There was Nazi propaganda that Polish nationals were conducting organised beatings of ethnic Germans, though I must say that I never witnessed this or heard of it in Bielsko-Biala. There was also muscular Polish propaganda about how strong Poland and its armed forces were. I particularly remember the slogan 'We'll be in Berlin in three days', which could be heard on the streets and seen on posters around the city.

It didn't quite work out that way.

Two

Occupied Poland

The dawn of 1 September 1939 saw Nazi Germany's Wehrmacht roll over the German-Polish frontier in what is now recognised as the start of World War II. The 'justified reason', according to Hitler, was the 'attack' by Polish military officers on the radio station in the Silesian city of Gleiwitz (today Gliwice) on 31 August.[1] History shows that that was a Nazi provocation; the 'Polish officers' weren't Poles at all, rather they were Nazi operatives furnishing an excuse for the invasion.[2] There was also a similar but separate incident on 3 September 1939, known as the Bromberg Bloody Sunday. The apparent massacre of Germans there was given as the reason by the Nazis to conduct 'reprisals' against the Poles. The killings and reprisals remain controversial and much debated by historians,[3] but later by chance I met a former Wehrmacht soldier who was one of the first members of the then German army to arrive on the scene. In 1953, he was one of my workmates and about to retire, but we spoke about the outbreak of the war and he told me about the incident. He was convinced that, like the Gleiwitz attack, this was a faked killing done by the Nazi regime as an excuse to initiate a reign of terror against the Poles. The impression he got from the situation as he arrived was that the 'German' victims were in fact Polish intellectuals and professionals from a concentration camp who had been killed by the Gestapo,[4] or other Nazi organisation. I have never been able to confirm this myself, but given what we now know it is certainly believable.

The war reaches Bielsko-Biala

In response to the Polish invasion, France and Great Britain pledged their assistance and on the morning of Sunday 3 September 1939 the then

British prime minister, Neville Chamberlain, made his now famous speech declaring that as the British government had received no undertaking by 11 a.m. (London time) that the Wehrmacht was withdrawing from Poland, Britain was at war with Nazi Germany.[5] Only an hour or two earlier on the same day, I had seen the first signs of war in Bielsko-Biala. At about 10 a.m. (Polish time) I saw three German soldiers walking up our street as I looked out the window. The one in the middle was carrying a machine gun; they were smiling and all three looked quite cheery.

During the previous evening of 2 September, I had heard some small arms and rifle fire for about half an hour and I had also seen some tracer bullets fly through the sky. My mother had warned to me to stay down and seek cover under the window. The local Polish forces had also blown up a train tunnel in the city in an effort to hamper the Wehrmacht's advance. Nonetheless, the sight of the German soldiers from my window on the morning of 3 September was the first I knew that war had broken out. I don't remember an announcement or seeing any reporting in the newspapers. The German community was, needless to say, quite happy, as they felt that they were now safe from harassment by the Polish.

The Wehrmacht had entered the city unopposed by the Polish army and the Polish population were quite surprised and shocked at what they saw: the German army driving through the city with trucks pulling weapons, such as the famous 88mm flak anti-aircraft gun, which was more powerful than they had expected. Some said openly, 'How on earth were we supposed to be able to fight all that?' For Poland, its elite forces remained its cavalry which had fought so effectively in the Polish-Russian war of 1919–21. The Wehrmacht in 1939 was much more modern and better equipped than Poland's armed forces and that – along with the Soviet Union's invasion from the east on 17 September – explains Poland's rapid defeat. Despite this, there are still a few myths and controversies going around. The German army, although mechanised, maintained their own cavalry and still used horses for transport,[6] and the academic research indicates that the Polish cavalry probably didn't charge German tanks with their lances as is still widely believed.[7] Having said that, many years later in Australia I met a chap called Hans at the South Australian German Club. He had been a tank commander at the time and he was certainly of the opinion that the Poles had used their lances against the

Panzers, even explaining how he and his crew shut the hatches to avoid injury. But perhaps this was an isolated incident. In any case, I'm sure the debate will continue.

One particular memory has stuck in my mind after all these years. A very short time before the war's outbreak, a Polish cavalry unit was conducting manoeuvres on a field just outside our city. After the exercise, the unit gathered in the field for a Catholic Mass. The Polish priest asked for God's blessing for the soldiers and their weapons, and that they be successful in battle through the death of their enemies. Coincidentally, after the German invasion, all the German troops – most of whom were from annexed Austria[8] (which was also strongly Catholic at the time) – also had a Catholic Mass. Like the Polish priest, the German priest asked for God's blessing for the soldiers and their weapons, and that they be successful in battle through the death of their enemies. Although I was only young at the time, seeing this fed my already growing scepticism towards religion. It all seemed quite odd given that Christianity, and indeed all major religions, preach that killing is a sin and against God's law.

The perils of 'friendly' fire: how I was wounded during the invasion

Having seen the German troops arrive, I found myself experiencing the invasion far more closely than I expected to or wanted to. Although the Wehrmacht had arrived at 10 a.m., they apparently had not been expected until about 2 p.m. that day. At about midday, a *Staffel* or squadron of the German air force (Luftwaffe) – which usually had about 12 aircraft – appeared over the city. My mother exclaimed, 'Look! Hermann Goering's Eagles are flying!' I looked up and saw the aircraft, and also a couple of black dots falling towards us. Blinded by the sun, I turned away but just as I stopped turning there was an explosion of dirt in front of me. I particularly remember seeing bricks thrown up by the explosion, which surprised me as the place we were standing was essentially farmland. In fact, grain had only recently been harvested from that exact spot.

After the dust had settled, I looked up and found myself only about two metres from the crater. I also saw my father lying about a foot from the crater and I wasn't sure if he was dead or not. My sister was also lying

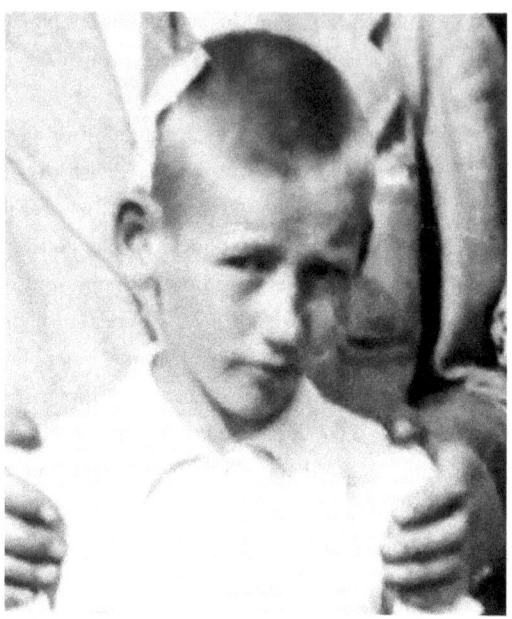

Me with the bandage that covered my head wound, 7 September 1939. (Otto Gaczol)

there and at first I feared the worst. But my father got up and brushed himself off unhurt and my sister, thankfully, was also uninjured. I think my father threw himself on top of her to shield her as the bombs struck. Before I knew it, I was standing there alone in the field as everyone quickly made for the safety of the nearest cellar. I, too, then went into the house but as I did I felt a warmth on my cheek. As I had been in the sun all of that morning, I thought it was a bit of sunburn. I descended the stairs into the cellar, where my mother was sitting in the corner. As soon as she saw me, she started to scream and at that moment I realised the warmth on my cheek was blood that had already started to coagulate.

My mother asked repeatedly, 'Are you all right? Are you all right? Your face is full of blood!' I said, 'Yes, I'm OK. I don't feel pain or anything.' I had really been quite lucky, and now consider 3 September to be my second birthday.

After a while, we all left the cellar and as I did I saw the victims of the air raid. In a case of 'friendly fire', seven German soldiers had been killed and a further 25 had been wounded. It was a strange experience, as I didn't feel anything emotionally except sympathy for the victims. But physically

I felt cold. Perhaps I experienced a mild state of shock. Morbidly curious, I went and had a look at them. To this day I can't explain what I saw. I'm guessing that they must have been killed by shrapnel of perhaps the overpressure of the explosion, as their bodies weren't dismembered or similarly ripped up – they were all essentially in one piece. One was lying on his back and looked as though he was asleep. Alongside his head, however, was his brain, but it was intact and it looked as though it had been carefully scooped out of his skull. Another soldier had the flesh on his leg split and the bone could be seen all the way through the thigh from the hip to the knee.

Eventually my mother dragged me away from the grisly spectacle and brought me to the attention of the German army doctor who was there. He cleaned the wound, made sure I was all right and then bandaged me to stop any further bleeding. The wound itself was on the upper head and the way he bandaged it made me look as if I were wearing a turban. After resting for a couple of days, I went out into the town with my friends and everywhere I went people would ask, 'Were you injured during the bombing?' In the end I got so sick of it I asked my mother to take the turban-like bandage off. She then put a much more subtle plaster on my head which remained there for the next week or so.

Our day-to-day lives

To provide some context for our lives under the occupation, our citizenship status probably needs to be explained, particularly given Upper Silesia's ethnic diversity, and the ideological and racial criteria that the Nazi regime applied. Upper Silesia and other regions such as Danzig were incorporated into the Third Reich itself, while the General Government (including the cities of Warsaw, Krakow, Radom and Lublin) was organised under a civilian governor-general, the Nazi party lawyer Hans Frank.[9] The *Deutsche Volksliste* was created to categorise the population as to who could or could not be assimilated into the Third Reich. It had four categories:

> *Volksdeutsche*: those persons who had actively demonstrated their Germanness culturally or politically before the war, such as through participation through German organisations;
>
> *Deutschstämmige*: persons of German descent who had not openly expressed their German identity during the interwar era;

Despite my parents' separation, this family portrait was taken in 1941. The dog was called Molly. (Otto Gaczol)

Eingedeutschte: persons suitable for 'Germanisation', meaning those persons of at least partial German descent or married to persons of German descent; and

Rückgedeutschte: persons of German descent who had been assimilated into Polish culture, but might be capable of 're-Germanisation'.[10]

The Gauleiter (district chief) of Upper Silesia, Josef Wagner, appears to have taken a more inclusive approach to the granting of 'German' status through the *Deutsche Volksliste* than other parts of occupied Poland.[11] Indeed, in eastern Upper Silesia, unlike most other parts of those regions annexed into the Third Reich, the authorities sought to include on the list as many residents as possible to avoid disrupting the region's crucial coal and steel industry. The Nazi authorities therefore applied enormous pressure on Upper Silesians to register for the list. By autumn 1943 they had classed 95 per cent of the region's population as Germans by placing them on the list, although 73 per cent were assigned to the low-ranked third category of *Eingedeutschte*.[12]

The first two categories allowed for acceptance as German citizens,[13] and we still have my mother's *Deutsche Volksliste* identification card which clearly states that acceptance. So, from our perspective, it was not an occupation. We saw it as a 'return to the Reich'. The Polish, of course, saw it as an occupation by a foreign power.

My mother also joined the Nazi Party in 1940. She did so in order to get work in a local winery. My mother didn't have to join the party as such, but not doing so meant she would not have landed that job. Being in the party meant that life was less difficult, as jobs, accommodation and making a living were all much easier to get if you joined. It was also the case that my mother had sympathies in that direction. As an example, when I was first sent to the German kindergarten after my parents' separation in 1935, she had a small swastika sewn into my blue uniform dust coat so that it could be identified as mine.

It might sound odd, but our lives as a family during the war were actually quite good. During October 1939, Antonina returned to Bielsko-Biala. On 9 November, my family moved into a new flat which had been given to Antonina. The flat was, by the standards of the time, modern and spacious with a kitchen and built-in toilet. I don't know what happened or why, but for some reason Antonina was in some way favoured by the Nazi authorities and this flat was some form of reward or perhaps compensation.

Later we found out that the flat had been expropriated from one of the city's Jews. He was terminally ill, perhaps with cancer, and the local Nazi occupation authorities had allowed him to stay in the building until he died, despite having expropriated the property. Years later, my mother was concerned that she had been seen as the actual owner of the flat and as a result she never returned to Bielsko-Biala as she feared some form of retribution.

Antonina, having been given this lovely new flat, was then denied a pension as the German authorities expected her to live off my mother's income. My mother, who occasionally had flashes of inspiration, came upon the idea of writing to Hitler directly to ask for a review of the decision. It was addressed 'Adolf Hitler, Reich Chancellor, Berlin' and I myself threw the letter in the mailbox. Sure enough, Antonina eventually received a rather miserly pension of 15 Reichsmarks per month. I collected it on her behalf as she was too old to do so herself. I very much doubt, however, that Hitler had anything to do with it personally.

At the winery, my mother worked in the sales department and every month she received three bottles of wine and a bonus bottle of brandy. My mother didn't drink, my father was gone and as children we didn't drink either, so she used to swap and barter the alcohol on the 'black

The only photo I have of my great-aunt Antonina, 1920s. (Otto Gaczol)

market' for other items to help make ends meet. I ended up getting a bicycle through one of these black market deals.

Antonina looked after my sister and me while my mother was at work and it was, for the most part, a good arrangement for all of us, although my great-aunt didn't inspire much affection from my sister as she was a rather forbidding character. Towards the end of the war, though, things got more difficult. Food was rationed and it got to the point where shopping became quite a chore.

Every morning we had to get up early so as to get milk at 7 a.m., and in some shops there were long queues even for basic items like potatoes and vegetables. Indeed, sometimes the queues were 20 or 30 metres long. I had to go along with my mother to help as she had a stiff elbow in one arm after it became infected years earlier when she was nursing my younger sister.

Our schooling essentially went on as before. Although we were given history lessons about Hitler, his life and his coming to power, we didn't really get any political indoctrination as such. In the mornings we were required to stand to attention when the teacher entered and say 'Heil Hitler!' but school was as normal as one could expect, with the usual lessons such as mathematics and language. There was also a strong emphasis on sport. The teachers themselves were of different ethnic backgrounds. Only two had German names while the others had either Polish or Czech names which, again, reflects the multi-ethnic nature of Upper Silesia. But given the circumstances and the times in which we lived, I think I ended up getting a very good education – better than some of those people I later met after the war in West Germany who had their education constantly interrupted by Allied air raids.

Eventually in 1944, my mother lost her job at the winery and began work at the Anker-Werke AG (Anchor Works) factory. Anker-Werke AG was then a Bielefeld-based company producing office machines, sewing machines and bicycles, though the factory in Bielsko-Biala did produce armaments. It went out of business in 1976. The company moved part of its operations to Bielsko-Biala in an effort to avoid Allied bombing raids and there were three sub-factories located in our city. Although I haven't been able to confirm it, my recollection is that one of the Bielsko-Biala factories produced components for the Lichtenstein radar units used by Luftwaffe night fighters.[14] I remember seeing the units being tested from the roof of the factory in which my mother worked. For security reasons, my mother wasn't allowed to talk about what they did there. A separate factory in the city not owned by Anker-Werke AG used to make artillery shells of various calibres which we could see by sneaking a peak through the wooden fence that surrounded the compound.

Despite the relatively small-scale war industry, we were reasonably safe, as Bielsko-Biala was too small and far away from the Allies to be a realistic bombing target for a major air raid, especially compared to the large industrial cities in the Ruhr valley in western Germany, or places like Hamburg.

Into the Hitler Youth

Before the war, I saw the Polish Boy Scouts marching around and I thought they looked very impressive in their uniforms with their hats that looked much like those the Canadian Mounties wore. After the occupation began, the Polish Scouts were abolished and replaced by Hitler Youth (*Hitler Jugend* or HJ), and its junior organisation for 10- to 14-year-olds called the *Deutsches Jungvolk* (DJ) or more colloquially as *Die Pimpfe*. Being in the HJ was all but compulsory until 1936. You could avoid it by not paying your fees, but after 1939 (or possibly 1941) it was compulsory for all boys over 10 years old.[15] Despite this, there were still boys in our town who weren't members. Perhaps it was different for the ethnic Germans (the *Volksdeutsche*) compared to the Reich itself, as the *Volksdeutsche* were effectively seen as second-class citizens. I myself was keen to join, and asked my mother if she could get some information for me or join me up, but she didn't and she didn't seem to care much. Despite this, I did eventually join the DJ in about May 1940.

Close to where we lived was a market square and on the corner was an empty house where the *Hitler Jugend Heim* (Hitler Youth home) was set up. On the square they had a stall and also had occasional marches and singing. One day that May, I walked past and was asked by the DJ man there if I'd like to join but, at only nine and a half, I said I was too young. He said, 'You're a big boy for your age – we can let you join,' and that's how I initially signed up.

The HJ proper was for those aged between 14 and 18, but I wanted to get in earlier if I could. I had a friend, Alfred or Alf, who thought he knew a way. The HJ was structured so as to develop future officers for the three services of the Wehrmacht: army (*Heer*); navy (*Kriegsmarine*); and air force (Luftwaffe). Alf was very keen to join the navy division, while I wanted to be in the Luftwaffe. But the HJ also had a band and in Bielsko-Biala they needed musicians – particularly trumpet and flute players. Alf was accepted into the HJ navy section through the direct route, but I had to get in using this charade. Eventually I was accepted as a flute player, even though I couldn't play a note. As I had a good quality uniform and they needed people to march in parades, I was signed-up and pretended to play the flute in those parades whenever the local Nazi Party *Bonzen*, or big shots, came to town.

For the first few years, we participated in all sorts of activities such as cut-price movies, camping and hiking. I really enjoyed it as there was lots of comradeship with singing and marching and you got much closer to your school friends. When we went out hiking, we stayed overnight in farm barns, sleeping on the hay. The *Hitler Jugend Heim* was an old school with some sports facilities, such as tennis courts. There, we would gather and receive what was essentially our political indoctrination. But we also got outdoor training, such as how to use a compass, outdoor orienteering using our wristwatches, and how to identify animal tracks such as those of hares, foxes and deer. Later, we were also taught how to shoot with a small-calibre rifle, and on 'army day' I got a chance to let off a burst of fire from an MG34 machine gun.

The HJ could also be quite brutal. I particularly remember when one of our members was thought to have stolen 10 Reichsmarks. Eventually the money was returned, but this chap had lied about it and the group leaders gave him quite a physical beating. While he was not permanently injured, it certainly was not something you would want to go through. I myself got into trouble with my own team members when a wisecrack to one of the leaders about it being 'time to go home' resulted in an extra half-hour of running and exercises. The other team members were very unhappy and started to make threats as we completed the exercises. 'The Holy Spirit is going to visit you,' they said, meaning that I could expect that, after dark, a blanket would be thrown over me, followed by a group beating. As it turned out, they either forgot about it or were just too tired to follow through on their threat. There was certainly a culture of physical punishment if you did something wrong but it wasn't arbitrary: you were only punished if you misbehaved, and if you could prove you were in the right, you were fine.

Despite my initial enthusiasm, the last couple of years saw the HJ lose its fun. It had settled into a routine of repetitive political and racial indoctrination, mostly centred on Hitler's life, which inevitably became boring. I got myself into trouble by continually staring out the window and more than once found myself doing the 'lap of honour': that is, running 20 laps of the school grounds as a punishment for not paying attention. It wasn't much of a punishment, really. The instructors couldn't see you for the entire duration and I spent most of my time walking, only breaking into a jog when I could be seen from the classroom windows. I remained in the HJ until Nazi Germany's military defeat in May 1945, when the Allied occupation forces disbanded it and declared it an illegal organisation as part of Germany's 'de-Nazification'.

What I experienced of the war

The 1930s and 1940s were, of course, the days before television and mass media as we know them today. Information was limited to newspapers as even radio wasn't widely available. After Antonina returned to Bielsko-Biala and we moved into the new flat, she also received one of the special radios that were then available – the *Volksempfänger* or people's receiver – but that could receive German channels only. Nonetheless, that's how we received our news, which came on nightly at about 10 o'clock. Daily reports told us the latest military developments and, in the last few months of the war, how far away the Red Army was. We had neighbours who listened to the BBC. This was, of course, illegal but we could hear it through the brick walls of the building and many people did it.

I remember some of the significant occasions of the war. For example, in 1940 I had to go to hospital for an operation. I remember that it was about that time that the invasion of France and the Benelux countries (Belgium, Netherlands and Luxembourg) occurred. When the Wehrmacht reached Paris and France capitulated, we had a school assembly where the headmaster gave a speech about the Wehrmacht's victory, and the flag of Nazi Germany was raised as a tribute to the victory.

Although our city was too small to suffer bombing itself, we did see US Army Air Force (USAAF) bombers overfly our area in an easterly direction during the last year of the war. I learnt later that the USAAF flew shuttle missions from Great Britain and Italy through to the Ukraine in the Soviet Union during June–September 1944 as part of Operation Frantic and it seems almost certain that it was these missions that we could see from Bielsko-Biala.[16] These shuttle missions did not last that long, but they flew almost every day in late 1944, as far as I can remember. The USAAF turned up at regular times of the day. For example, for a period they arrived at 10 a.m., but then that changed to 12 noon for a few weeks. Our school times were then built around their routine. They were easy to count as they always flew in box formations with a prescribed number of aircraft.[17]

On one occasion I counted 700 aircraft flying eastwards, and just one left the formation to attack an oil refinery about 10 kilometres from Bielsko-Biala. A few minutes later, a white cloud rose into the air, indicating that the refinery had been hit. The cloud eventually turned to black and the refinery continued to burn for three days.[18]

On another unusual occasion, the air raid siren sounded 'all clear' and we left our cellars with one single B-17 bomber still circling our city. It eventually dropped some propaganda leaflets. Although it was forbidden to read them, I managed to get a glimpse of one before an adult snatched it from my hand. It said that the Wehrmacht had surrendered in Italy. I remember it being in late summer 1944 and it may have been the time when the Allied armies had captured Rome in June/July of that year.

Apart for the USAAF, who always flew during the day, there were also a few night raids but as it was dark and we were hiding in the cellar I don't know if these were British raids or the Soviet air force. After the famous Dambusters raid by the Royal Air Force's 617 Squadron on the night of 16–17 May 1943, we had some barrage balloons deployed near our city as there was a dam in the hills above Bielsko-Biala. These balloons were inflated before the USAAF arrived and we watched for them as they served as an early warning to us of an impending raid along with the air raid sirens.

As someone who lived close to my school – it was up at the end of my street – I was required to come to the school as a fire warden. Initially when an air raid warning was sounded, the other wardens and I were required to go to the school and protect it from fire. Everybody over the age of 12 was trained in first aid and we were issued a helmet and a gas-mask and, for a time, we were even required to sleep at the school, but that was eventually changed as we had no chance to do our homework.

At the end of the corridors were water buckets and a pump and a huge box of sand, which were to be used to extinguish any fires that broke out. Two wardens were stationed on each floor. At first we were instructed to open all the windows, but later that was changed to keeping them closed as the authorities realised that closed windows would better deny oxygen to any fires that broke out. The other change of policy was that the children, who were initially instructed to stay at the school during an air raid, were then sent home when an air raid warning sounded. This was in response to experiences in western Germany where some schools were hit during Allied air raids and children killed as they had been sheltering there. Despite our efforts, what we as school fire wardens had been given was not adequate to fight the fires that developed during these air raids. The magnesium-based incendiary bombs used by the Allies couldn't be extinguished with water. Even sand was problematic, as the Allies eventually began using bombs filled with multiple incendiaries that spread out in all directions.[19] There was just no way that we, as child fire wardens, were going to be able to extinguish them all.

Thankfully, we were never put to the test. Bielsko-Biala accepted about 10,000 people as evacuees for the Reich proper when the Allied bombing of German cities intensified. One of the women was from Cologne and had survived the 1,000-plane raid. On the night of 30–31 May 1942, the RAF despatched 1,046 aircraft to bomb the city of Cologne in the Rhine-Ruhr valley. Firestorms took hold and almost 2.5 square kilometres of the city were laid waste, including 13,000 homes.[20] One evening, a woman was watching a short propaganda film in the cinema about how to fight fires in an air raid and, given that she had experienced the reality, began to laugh at how inadequate the film was. Someone informed the Gestapo and she was brought in for questioning. When asked about her behaviour, she simply said, 'I was in Cologne,' and with that she was released without any further ado.

The 'real' Germans evacuated from the Reich, however, looked down upon us *Volksdeutsche* and insulted us with names like 'Polaks'. Perhaps because of this, or perhaps not, the woman from Cologne stole the linen from her neighbour when she eventually left Bielsko-Biala.

During the time when the school was still used as a shelter, I was also a designated messenger. After the roll call was complete and the number of people sheltering at the school established, it was my job to run to the winery where my mother was working to report the final numbers of students and teachers to the local authorities. My mother volunteered to work on the switchboard during the air raids and I got myself into trouble occasionally by reporting the numbers directly to her rather than through one of the winery workers who acted as the senior warden.

One of the strangest things I remember is about my school friend, Edmund. His father was a soldier in the Wehrmacht and he was full of stories that sounded extraordinary at the time but were, for the most part, later proved to be right. One day he came to school and excitedly announced, 'The Germans have got a rifle that shoots around corners!'

We all laughed at him and asked how something like that was possible. But sure enough, many years later I discovered that the German army had indeed invented a mechanism through which a rifle with a curved barrel could shoot around corners.[21]

Another day he arrived and started to talk about a bomb that was guided by copper wires and would always hit its target. I didn't believe it and even argued with him but again he was right: the Luftwaffe did have a wire-guided bomb that could hit targets with a high degree of accuracy[22] and they were the precursors of today's precision guided munitions (PGMs). Another one of his stories was of a rocket-powered aircraft that launched rockets against enemy aircraft. Again, it was true: the Bachem Ba 349 'Natter', which was an experimental rocket-powered vertical take-off interceptor, was being developed at the time.[23] Finally, he told us about some newly developed night-vision equipment, which was again true.[24]

I always kept asking where he got these stories from but he always fudged the answer, saying something like, 'Oh, I just heard it somewhere…' All I can think is that he had a family member who was somehow involved in the various secret projects that were going on during the war. If that was the case, then that family member may have drunk too much, and certainly talked too much.

Polish life in occupied Bielsko-Biala

The Poles themselves seemed to pragmatically accept the occupation and went about their business as best they could. Initially at least, some of the Poles in my town even went as far as to say, 'We now have law and order here!'

On a day-to-day level, there was no discrimination amongst people of the Polish communities and German communities themselves, from what I could see. For example, my mother was at one stage in charge of the canteen at the Anker-Werke AG factory during Christmas 1944. According to her, all the staff got a kilogram of venison as a Christmas gift and both the Poles and the Germans were treated equally when they ate at that canteen. The Poles also received extra ration coupons when doing heavy physical work. On our street, I can remember there were both Poles and

Germans, and on a day-to-day level everything was quite normal. They spoke German, but at times also spoke Polish, and no one really cared.

Despite what seemed to me at the time to be a relatively benign environment for the Poles in my town, the historic reality must be acknowledged. Occupied Poland suffered terribly during the occupation by Nazi Germany – more than any other country except, perhaps, the Soviet Union.[25] Under Nazi 'race theory', the Poles were seen as Slavic 'subhumans' and were treated accordingly. Many studies have showed that about six million Polish died at the hands of the Nazi regime, and many more were deported into the Third Reich to work as slave labourers. Further, there were many forced deportations and resettlements – what today is called ethnic cleansing – throughout occupied Poland, including Upper Silesia.[26]

The Soviets, too, were quite brutal. Most notoriously, they murdered approximately 22,000 officers of the Polish armed forces in the Katyn forest region. The Soviets eventually admitted to this crime in 1990, having previously tried to blame Nazi Germany.[27] Incidentally, there was an Adolf Jozef Gaczol listed amongst the Katyn victims but as far as we know there is no relationship to my family.[28]

Even in Bielsko-Biala, if there were any issues with the Poles, they were dealt with swiftly and sometimes ruthlessly by the Nazi authorities. One of my Polish friends, Frank, was employed at the Anker-Werke AG plant where my mother worked. We played together a lot before the war. One day I came home to see my mother and Frank's mother on the street talking in front of our home. Having not seen Frank for some time, I asked how he was. I was shocked to find that he was dead. Even worse, he had been killed by the Nazi authorities for having taken three days off work because he was sick. As he didn't have permission and hadn't phoned to let the factory know, he was arrested and sent to Auschwitz, where he was killed. I was stunned, as he had been a great friend, and I was also deeply sad and embarrassed.

There was also, of course, the reality that many of the worst Nazi death camps, such as Auschwitz, were located within occupied Poland and many Poles – both Jewish and non-Jewish – met their fates there. Auschwitz itself was about 30 kilometres north-west of Bielsko-Biala and I certainly have memories of that.

The Jews of Bielitz, and Auschwitz

The Nazi regime had slowly but surely established its persecution of Jews and other minorities in the Third Reich before invading Poland in 1939. Already in March 1933, the *Schutzstaffel* (SS), Hitler's 'elite guard', established a concentration camp outside the town of Dachau for political opponents of the regime. On 1 April of that year, the Nazis organised a nationwide boycott of Jewish-owned businesses in Germany and many local boycotts continued throughout much of the 1930s. Just one week later, the Law for the Restoration of the Professional Civil Service, which excluded Jews and political opponents from university and governmental positions was passed. Similar laws enacted in the following weeks affected Jewish lawyers, judges, doctors, and teachers. On 10 May 1933, the now notorious book burning occurred in Berlin and throughout Germany. Laws against gypsies, homosexuals, Jehovah's Witnesses all followed and in September 1935, the Nuremberg Laws were passed which made Jews second-class citizens. On 9 November 1938, in a nationwide pogrom called Kristallnacht (Crystal Night or Night of Broken Glass), the Nazis and their collaborators burned synagogues, looted Jewish homes and businesses, and killed at least 91 Jews. Approximately 30,000 Jewish men were imprisoned in the Dachau and other concentration camps and several hundred Jewish women also were imprisoned in local jails.[29]

So when the Wehrmacht arrived in Bielsko-Biala on 3 September 1939, the Nazi regime was already well-practised at identifying the Jewish and other minority populations for arrest, persecution and deportation. On 4 September 1939, the Nazis burned down the two synagogues in Bielsko and the Ḥ.N. Bialik Jewish cultural home. A few days later they burned down the two synagogues in the then separate town of Biala, and its Orthodox Jews were forced to throw the Holy Books into the fire. The summer of 1940 saw a ghetto established but it was then liquidated in June 1942 when the town's remaining Jewish population was deported to Auschwitz.[30]

By coincidence there is a famous biography of a Jewish resident of Bielsko-Biala which details the Jewish experience of the city's occupation. Gerda Weissmann-Klein was born in Bielsko-Biala in 1924 and was 15 years old when the Wehrmacht occupied Poland. Initially she and her family lived in the basement of her childhood home for nearly three years, but she was then separated from her parents, who were sent to Auschwitz. Having spent the next three years in a succession of labour camps, she and the other inmates were sent on a five-month, 500-kilometre death march under SS guard. Of the more than 2,000 women subjected to exposure, starvation and arbitrary execution, fewer than 120 were alive when they were found by American soldiers in Czechoslovakia.[31] Her biography, *All But My Life*, was first published in 1957. The book was reissued in the mid-1990s and a documentary was also made at that time entitled *One Survivor Remembers*.[32]

I was not a witness to the more dramatic aspects of the persecution such as the burning of the synagogues, though I did see their burnt-out shells afterwards. I, however, did see that before their removal to the ghettos and then to Auschwitz and other concentration camps, the Jewish population were already being exploited and abused by doing the city's dirty work such as garbage removal and street cleaning. Initially, the Jews were required to wear thin white armbands showing they were Jews, but they would roll their sleeves up so you couldn't see them. Then they were required to wear the yellow Star of David with the word '*Jude*' (Jew) written on it. This continued until they slowly disappeared from the city. After 1943, I didn't see any more Jews in Bielsko-Biala.

Auschwitz was, of course, the largest Nazi concentration camp and death camp and has since become a byword for the Holocaust itself. Initially a Polish army barracks, 'Auschwitz' ultimately became a large complex that encompassed a series of camps run by the SS and took its name after the village (Oswiecim in Polish) outside of which it was built. Three main camps were established: Auschwitz I in May 1940; Auschwitz II (also called Auschwitz-Birkenau) in early 1942; and Auschwitz III (also called Auschwitz-Monowitz) in October 1942.[33] Of these three, Auschwitz-Birkenau was deliberately established as a death camp after the fate of the European Jews under Nazi occupation was decided in Berlin at the Wannsee Conference in January 1942.[34]

The first stories we heard about Auschwitz were that political prisoners were being taken there as part of their 're-education' to be 'good' Nazis. Curious, I suggested to some of my friends that we grab our bicycles and ride the 30 kilometres or so to take a look. My friends were keen, but we thought it would probably be a good idea if we checked with the local HJ authorities if this was all right. We were told very directly and menacingly that this was not going to happen and that we were to stay away from Auschwitz otherwise we would find ourselves in huge trouble. So, we didn't go and we never spoke about it again. It had become a taboo subject.

Slowly we heard through word of mouth that Auschwitz was going to become a concentration camp. Stories about the Jews and their fate came later on and only slowly – piece by piece. While there has been much discussion about what the German population knew of the camps and what went on there, the stories we heard were accepted as facts and as the war progressed we knew about what was going on there. This includes the stories of torture, removal of hair, removal of jewellery and gold teeth, the gas chambers and the other 'activities' – it was common knowledge.

Strangely enough, it was Edmund at school who spread the stories about the murder of the Jews. He would come to school saying things like 'Do you know what they are doing to the Jews at Auschwitz? They are killing the Jews and making soap out of them!' Indeed, part of our rations included soap and for a time we received some poor-quality soap that floated on water. Eventually stories began to circulate that this soap was indeed made from Jews and people very quickly stopped buying it. After a short while, the soap disappeared from the markets. This has been a controversial debate over recent years and while the Auschwitz-Birkenau museum eventually concluded that a small experimental amount of soap – between 10 and 100 kilograms – was produced in Gdansk/Danzig,[35] it also appears that none was manufactured in Auschwitz itself, nor was it ever produced on an industrial scale for general use by the population.[36]

Although I heard these rumours and stories through Edmund, the adults seldom if ever talked about Auschwitz and what was happening there. The impression I had was that people didn't like what was happening but were too afraid to say anything out of fear of persecution and possibly ending up there themselves. Indeed, on my trip to Australia, one of my fellow German passengers called Gerhardt told me that his brother had worked in Auschwitz in the camp office and had made a complaint about what was occurring. Gerhardt's brother was told very quickly by his boss to keep his views to himself otherwise he would find himself as an inmate. In the scraps of conversation I overheard between Antonina and my mother, they didn't approve either, even though my mother was a member of the Nazi Party. Having experienced good business relationships with the Jewish community during the time my family owned the bakery, they couldn't understand why the Jews were being persecuted and killed the way they were.

One final point to be made is that despite the fact that the USAAF was bombing other targets such as oil refineries in Upper Silesia, Auschwitz was never the target of a deliberate Allied attack.[37] I do, however, remember the camp being hit by mistake during a USAAF air raid on 13 September 1944.[38] Apparently stray bombs accidentally hit an SS barracks (killing 15 guards), a slave labour workshop (killing 40 prisoners), and the railroad track leading to the gas chambers.[39] Although the camp was 30 kilometres away, some of the bombs fell near our city – we could feel the mild vibrations of the explosions through the building. I remember it specifically because, although we were sheltering in the cellar, my mother was trying to cope with the stress by telling jokes but was told off by Antonina. She had instead been praying and saying how ridiculous it was for my mother to be testing her comedic skills when we could all be dead in the next 10 minutes.

My father and his fate

After my parents' separation, my father remained distant from us. He found a new job as a pastry baker in a shop just off the main city square. He visited once a week to pay his alimony but that was the limit of our contact. Despite my desire to spend time with him, it seemed he didn't really want me around. I remember once in winter I had wanted to play a bit and started a snow fight by throwing a snowball at him. Instead of responding in a playful way, he got very angry and threw me down into a ditch. There were also occasions when he hit my mother. I then began to withdraw from him. In the last few years, I only saw him once every six months or so, though on a few occasions he slept in the spare room when he was in town.

The last time I saw him was during the summer of 1944. At that stage he lived and worked in a nearby city not far from Gliwice (Gleiwitz) called Bytom (Beuthen) which was about 70 kilometres away from Bielsko-Biala. My mother had asked him to make a large birthday cake – what in German is called a *Torte* – and she gave me one or two bottles of wine as payment and sent me by myself on the train to Beuthen/Bytom to pick it up. I still remember that cake. It was particularly impressive as it had a small figure of a black man sitting on its edge dressed in a multicoloured suit. He also wore a turban with a feather in it and in his arms he was holding a huge red rose made of marzipan. Then, on each side of him, it had more red roses that slowly decreased in size as they got further away from the man until they joined up on the opposite side of the cake.

It was during this last visit that my father told me what he thought of the war. Although he was not really a political person, he did on that occasion say to me, 'Hitler is not going to win this war. He's made too many enemies.' Having been indoctrinated into the HJ and other Nazi propaganda, I was not very happy to hear him say this.

Like my mother, my father probably signed up to the *Deutsche Volksliste* but unlike my mother it is likely that he signed up purely out of pragmatism, as not signing possibly meant being sent to a concentration camp.[40] Also, being on the list made getting employment easier. His alimony payments book has his name spelt as 'Thaddäus Gatschol': that is, in a Germanised way, rather than with a Polish 'cz', which again probably indicates his inclusion on the *Deutsche Volksliste*. The downside of this was that as a member of the *Deutsche Volksliste* he was eligible to be conscripted into the Wehrmacht. These are the logical conclusions I have come to, as he was drafted, at the age of 37, just after I last saw him.

Our information about him is very patchy as it relies on family word of mouth and distant memories of long-ago conversations. Most of what I know comes from what I overheard in conversations between my mother and Antonina. But as best we know, he was, apparently, initially stationed in Denmark in an artillery regiment and was then transferred to the grenadiers (infantry). In November 1944 we received an official letter saying that he was missing in action in the vicinity of Krakow, which is about 120 kilometres from Bielsko-Biala. My mother never told my sister or me about my father or what happened to him. I only found out many years later through a family friend that my father was killed in action – possibly as late as January 1945. We still have that alimony payments booklet that shows a final entry of 40 Reichsmarks being recorded in late January 1945. Later, we went to the various German authorities such as the German Red Cross, the Federal Archives (*Bundesarchiv*), the German Service Personnel Records Organisation (*Deutsche Dienststelle*) and the German War Graves Commission (*Volksbund*) requesting whatever information they had. They found nothing – not even his draft papers. So, sadly, the alimony payments booklet and a few photos are the only pieces of evidence we have of him.

Our last days in Bielsko-Biala

The second half of 1944 was a triumph for the Allies and disastrous for the Wehrmacht. In the south, Rome fell to the western Allies in June 1944. That same month, the western Allies landed in Normandy on D-Day. Also in June, a major assault by the Red Army resulted in the collapse of the Wehrmacht's Army Group Centre which was at least as catastrophic as the defeat at Stalingrad 18 months earlier, perhaps even worse.[41] August saw the destruction of a large part of the German army in the west in the Falaise pocket,[42] and Paris was liberated on 25 August. By mid-December, the western Allies had arrived at the Rhine River and the Red Army had reached the border of the Reich itself at East Prussia. The Wehrmacht's last gasp counter-offensive in the west – the Battle of the Bulge – started in mid-December 1944 and by mid-January 1945 it had ground to a halt having exhausted the army's reserves of fuel and armour.

We kept up to date with the general news and the Red Army's advance through radio broadcasts. At first, with the Red Army 100 kilometres from Bielsko-Biala, I wasn't too alarmed until Edmund said, 'Are you kidding? They could be here in two hours!' At that moment, a wave of terror hit me. Through Nazi propaganda we had heard that the Red Army was brutal in its advance and I began to ask my mother serious questions about what we were going to do.

My father's prophecy about Hitler having made too many enemies had come true.

Three

Flight from the Red Army

On 12 January 1945, the Red Army's offensive against the Wehrmacht opened in southern Poland, starting from their bridgehead over the Vistula River near Sandomierz only 240 kilometres from Bielsko-Biala. On 17 January 1945, Warsaw fell to the Soviets and on 19 January the Red Army's spearheads reached the Silesian frontier of pre-war Germany. By 31 January 1945, the Red Army was at Küstrin, on the lower Oder, only 40 miles from Berlin.[1]

The Russians are coming

With news of the Red Army's success filtering through, people were already trying to leave Upper Silesia in late 1944 and early January 1945. Although Edmund's warning about the Russians had been a wake-up call, the reality really struck when one day just before school, a German *Feldwebel* (army sergeant) and the school janitor came to our classroom and declared the school closed until the end of the war as it was being taken over by the Wehrmacht for use as barracks.

At first I was thrilled at the idea of no more school but then the gravity of the situation hit me: the war had again reached Bielsko-Biala, but this time from the other direction through the advance of a hostile Red Army. I was terrified and went home to ask my mother about what we were going to do. I wanted to leave as soon as possible. When she arrived home, she also realised the seriousness of the situation and said she would start to organise our departure immediately.

Although Nazi propaganda stories were exaggerated, at their core was a fundamental truth: having been murdered and brutalised themselves through Nazi Germany's invasion,[2] the Red Army were, at least to some degree, intent on revenge. Although they saw themselves as liberators rather than conquerors, they were determined to gather what they saw as 'the spoils of war'. Stories of rape were legion and to this day no one can truly ascertain the extent of the Red Army's violation of women as they advanced through eastern Europe and into Germany.[3] Estimates of women raped in Berlin alone are normally around the 100,000 mark and when one takes into account the eastern territories such as East Prussia and Pomerania the overall figure is possibly up to two million.[4]

The Red Army also had little compassion for German prisoners of war[5] and German teenagers who they saw as either a potential threat, or as a labour resource for the Soviet Union. I heard later that when the Red Army arrived in Bielsko-Biala, the local Polish authorities gave them a list of all the German schoolchildren, and any boy over the age of 14 was arrested and taken back to Siberia. One of my schoolmates, Günter, was taken away and he died in the Soviet Union. Edmund was also one of those arrested and taken away. Although he returned after two years, he died shortly afterward due to the poor conditions under which he was held. A third school friend, Stanislaw, also returned. In 1988, I met him again and although he was only one year older than me, he was physically shattered – he could hardly walk and couldn't eat any solid food.[6]

So it was with good reason that we feared the Red Army's advance and made our plans to go west and try to meet up with the armies of the western Allies as they advanced into Nazi-occupied Europe from France and the other liberated western European countries.

Divided we fled

On 22 January 1945, my mother told us that we were all going to leave Bielsko-Biala, but that she would be evacuating with her company to Bielefeld and that my sister and I would be travelling separately with Antonina. The idea was that we would eventually meet up in the German-speaking region of the now Czech Republic called the Sudetenland, which had been annexed by Nazi Germany in September/October 1938 following the Munich Conference.

The plan was very simple: the three of us would go to the station and catch a train to wherever it was going as long as it allowed us to avoid any

My mother, centre in light-coloured blouse, on the Anker-Werke AG evacuation train from Bielsko-Biala to Bielefeld, late January 1945. (Otto Gaczol)

Soviet entanglements. I was a little stunned to hear that we were going to separate. My mother explained that Anker-Werke AG had a train on which the company would transport its machinery back to Bielefeld and that she had gotten herself a place on that train. I don't know whether she asked if we could travel as a family together but I know that she was not the only person to be evacuated with her company. Indeed, I still have a photo of my mother sitting in a rail carriage with others. So the three of us left on 22 January and my mother left two days later on 24 January.

On 27 January 1945, the Red Army reached Upper Silesia and in the process liberated Auschwitz.[7] This date is now commemorated as International Holocaust Remembrance Day.[8] Bielsko-Biala was occupied during 10–12 February and from what I heard, there were, apart from a few beatings here and there, few revenge attacks against the Germans who had stayed there.[9]

At the main train station in Bielsko-Biala, we went to the main goods terminal rather than the passenger platforms. There we found two Nazi officials, one of whom tried to block our way to the train saying that it was only for those from his particular district of the city. But the other official was someone Antonina knew, and she persuaded him to tell the first official to allow us on the train.

Main train station, Bielsko-Biala, from which we left in January 1945. Photo taken in 2009. (Andrew Gaczol)

Our first travel leg lasted for 48 hours and on the first day it was reasonably comfortable with a warm carriage and some food we had brought with us from home. But after the first day the heating system on the train failed so it got cold and uncomfortable and gave us little chance to get some proper sleep. The windows were frozen closed and covered with a thin layer of ice. Apart from the frigid conditions, my other concern was the Allied air forces. By this stage, the Luftwaffe had all but ceased to be an effective fighting force and the western Allies particularly were able to roam into German airspace at will. In order to hinder the operations of the German army, they were attacking trains and other forms of ground transport regardless of their purpose.[10]

My 'marvellous' time in Herrlich

After those two days, we arrived in the Sudetenland at a small but pleasant town called Duchcov (Dux) about 80 kilometres directly south of Dresden. We were unloaded from the train and carried our things to a school where we were to be accommodated. We had arrived at about 7 a.m. or 8 a.m. We were cold, tired and hungry but were given something to eat, a chance to wash and the opportunity to sleep on straw that had been spread on the floor. In the evening we were taken by bus to a small village called Hrdlovka[11] – which ironically in German (Herrlich) means gorgeous or marvellous – a very short distance west of Duchcov (Dux). There, we spent four or five days in another school but this one had proper beds and good food. For no apparent reason, Antonina gave me a rough time. It was so bad that at one stage the other refugees started to tell her to leave me alone. Even on the train, she had told me off on one occasion for not getting her a cup of sufficiently hot water for her tea. From her point of view, the below-zero temperatures were just another one of my 'excuses'.

In the evening, the three of us were split up and allocated to some foster families. Antonina went with a family who lived above a huge hall – possibly an old cinema – where she was given a small room with a bed, set of drawers and basic cooking facilities with which to look after herself. My sister ended up with a family who owned a small haberdashery business. They were lovely people who really thought my sister was wonderful. They even offered to adopt her should my mother have gone missing on her way west. My sister settled in very well and was given little privileges such as new clothes. One day I went around their house to see her and she was in the middle of eating a piece of cake, which at that time was a luxury. Knowing I'd ask for some, she stuffed it in her mouth as quickly as she could, almost managing to lose half of it on the floor. Afterwards, we both broke out in laughter.

My foster family in Hrdlovka (Herrlich), the Eckerts, were also friendly and welcoming, particularly my foster-mother, Hedwig. Herr Eckert was in the Nazi *Sturmabteilung*[12] (SA, more commonly known as stormtroopers). They had been Hitler's street-fighters in the 1930s when the Nazis were seeking power, regularly getting into brawls with the German communists and other Nazi Party opponents. Herr Eckert's SA membership was, however, almost comical as he was very quiet and looked like he couldn't hurt a fly. Like my mother, he probably joined the Nazi Party in order to get or keep his job as foreman in the local coal mines. I hardly spoke with him for the three months I was there. Hedwig, on the other hand, was wonderful despite also being a committed Nazi. Whereas my great aunt and even my mother treated me still as a child and were quick to criticise, Hedwig treated me as an adult and let me do as I pleased as long as I obeyed a few simple rules such as being home for dinner and obeying a 9 p.m. curfew. The rest of the family consisted of two children: a son and daughter.

The son, Rolf, was only 16 years old; he was in the army and was essentially a radar operator in an anti-aircraft unit equipped with 88mm flak guns. Through good luck, he was stationed near his home village and would come home periodically to see his family. I must admit the first time I met him I was a little taken aback. Wearing an army winter overcoat and with a shock of blond hair, he walked into the room where I was reading. But even though he was two years older than me, he was shorter than I was and so skinny that with the overcoat on he looked like a scarecrow. I thought to myself that if boys his age and his size were fighting in the army, then Germany must be truly desperate for manpower.[13]

The daughter, Margrit, was 20 years old and had been engaged to an officer who had been killed on the eastern front. Magrit was supposed to be coming to visit us and my foster-mother was very excited and looking forward to introducing me to her. But the visit never happened. Margit lived in Dresden and became a victim of the controversial bombing of 13–14 February 1945 when Britain's Royal Air Force destroyed almost the entire city in a single air raid, with a death toll of 25,000 people.[14] Margit was missing after the raid and was almost certainly killed. Earlier, Frau Eckert had asked me to help her make some cushions for Margit out of some HJ scarves when all of a sudden she stopped and said, 'Oh, they're black. I can't send her a black cushion. It's a bad sign.' I thought she was being ridiculously superstitious and we sent the cushions about a week before the raid. While I'm sure our cushions had nothing to do with her fate, the fact is her family never saw her again.

It was at about that time that I also found myself being 'volunteered' for the armed wing of the SS: the Waffen SS. One of the other boys from Bielsko-Biala who had been evacuated to Hrdlovka (Herrlich) was determined to join the army to get away from his family, with whom he didn't get on. After getting permission from his father, he presented himself to the recruiting authorities at Duchcov (Dux) and I waited patiently for him outside the office while his application was being processed. After a while, my friend came out of the office accompanied by a decorated German army major who had his arm draped over my friend's shoulder. The major approached me directly and said, 'So, I hear you want to join the Waffen SS!' I was both stunned and mortified, as the Waffen SS were elite fighting units ideologically committed to the Nazi regime and, although effective in a military sense, they were fanatical and suffered extremely high casualty rates.[15] They also took part in some of the regime's worst atrocities, such as the massacre at Oradour-sur-Glane.[16] For a moment I stood there speechless, but eventually I pulled myself together and stammered, 'I'm sorry, Herr Major, but I want to join the Luftwaffe.' I was scared that he still might be able to conscript me regardless, so I was relieved when he replied, 'Oh, that's all right then,' and turned round and went back into the office. Luckily I was still 14. Had I been 16, he probably would have drafted me. In any case, I was furious with my friend and said, 'If I keep hanging around with you, I'm going to find myself in the army and get killed!' Wisely, I decided not to spend much more time with him.

Despite being a German evacuee, I did make friends with some of the local Czech boys. There were a couple of Czechs who used to play marbles under the kitchen window of our flat. One day I went downstairs and they called over to me in German and asked if I wanted to join in. I had no idea how to play their game, but I went over to them and we became good friends. One of them, Pepik, lived in my building. Eventually we spent a fair bit of time together, going to the movies, playing football and generally what one would call today 'hanging out'.

Without question there were tensions between the Czechs and the Germans with prejudices on both sides. On one occasion, I was with my Czech friends, who had made a small boat and wanted to test it in the local lake. They introduced me to some other Czech boys but nothing was said. At that moment, another Czech boy came along with two young German guys who I knew from Silesia – Hans and Manfred – who had just arrived as evacuees. The Czech called out to their compatriot, 'Why are you bringing those bloody Germans here?' A little embarrassed, my Czech friends said, 'But Otto is German…' to which they replied, 'Yeah, but Otto is all right.' Similarly, when I later caught up with the two German boys, they asked me, 'Why are you hanging out with Czechs?' It didn't bother me in the slightest as the Czech guys and I got on fine and, being a stranger, I was grateful for the company. The only awkward moment came when one day my Czech friends asked whether I thought

Hitler was going to win the war. My instinctive response was 'You've got to be joking! The war must be almost over: the Russians are on their way!' But given the level of paranoia and suspicion at the time, I fudged an answer, saying, 'I don't know what Hitler is going to do and there is nothing I can do about it.' Indeed, any talk of defeat was likely to see some form of punishment from the Nazi authorities.

Day-to-day, life in Hrdlovka (Herrlich) was relatively uneventful. School was only three days a week – Monday, Wednesday and Friday – and I can't say that I learnt much during my time there. The only real excitement came when a German fighter aircraft came down near the village and I was called into duty as a runner or messenger. I had volunteered to be a runner and that day was given a message that I was required to report to the police station, which I did. I was tasked with finding out what had happened to the pilot and passing the information back to the authorities. I had already seen and heard the aircraft – a Focke-Wulf 190 – circling the village that morning. When I caught up with the 24-year-old pilot, who by now was being assisted by a couple of farmers, he explained to me that he had been chased down by five USAAF fighters but had managed to escape. Unsure of whether he was still in German airspace or that of the enemy, he had circled our town's train station trying to read the name so that he could orient himself. However, with his fuel running low, he had to belly land the aircraft. Interesting as it was, that was the only time I was called upon to fulfil my duties as a messenger.

In about mid to late April 1945, I found myself joining the Werewolves with my friends Hans and Manfred. The Werewolves were supposed to be an underground resistance movement made up of SS and HJ members who were going to take the fight up to the invading Allied armies through various forms of sabotage behind the lines.[17] The other option for us was to join the *Volkssturm*, which was a sort of improvised home guard of old war veterans and young HJ members. In hindsight it must be said that it was the bottom of the barrel in terms of Nazi Germany's manpower. I had no intention of joining them, as I was thoroughly sick of being ordered around by adults and the Werewolves sounded much more glamorous. Having signed up, we were ordered to present ourselves for two weeks' training at a camp near Duchcov (Dux). When we arrived, we saw the commander, who was a well decorated army *Feldwebel* with two tank patches on his arm indicating that he had single-handedly destroyed two enemy tanks. To my eyes, however, it looked terribly undisciplined, as the recruits we could see weren't following orders appropriately. Inside the office, we were told that the camp had been fully booked and that we had to wait until the next call-up. But the next call-up never came and that was the end of my career as a Werewolf. As it turned out, the Werewolves were mostly propaganda bluster that showed very few real results.

It was also at about that time we received a new HJ leader. A 20-year-old former Panzer crew member, he had lost a leg below the knee when his tank ran over a mine. He was very pleasant and we all very much liked him.

Escape to the west

As the Red Army continued to advance, it became apparent that the Nazi regime had entered its final days. During our last days in Hrdlovka (Herrlich), Rolf went to a restaurant in the village to use the bathroom. In it, he overheard two Czechs speaking about the war and mentioned that Hitler was dead. Surprised, he went back home and told the family and they all gathered around the radio to see if there was any news. There was nothing. So he then returned to his anti-aircraft unit and asked there. Again, nothing had been heard. Twenty-four hours later, the news did come through. It had been announced at about 10.30 p.m. (German time) 1 May 1945.[18] How those two Czechs in the restaurant knew, I have no idea.

On 8 May we heard of Nazi Germany's surrender to the Allied forces. Although no one panicked as such, there were many nervous people, including me. The uncertainty as to what was going to happen to us all generated a lot of anxiety. I certainly wasn't courageous enough to travel westwards by myself but as it happened our HJ leader took the initiative. He told us that the following morning – 9 May – he was going to head westwards towards the American lines. His offer was clear: 'I don't want to see any of you fall into Russian hands, and while I can't take responsibility for you, I will lead you towards the Americans. This is strictly voluntary. You don't have to come but you can if you want to.'

I decided to go with our new HJ leader, but in order to convince my foster-mother to let me go, I told her a lie that, as a Werewolf, I had been

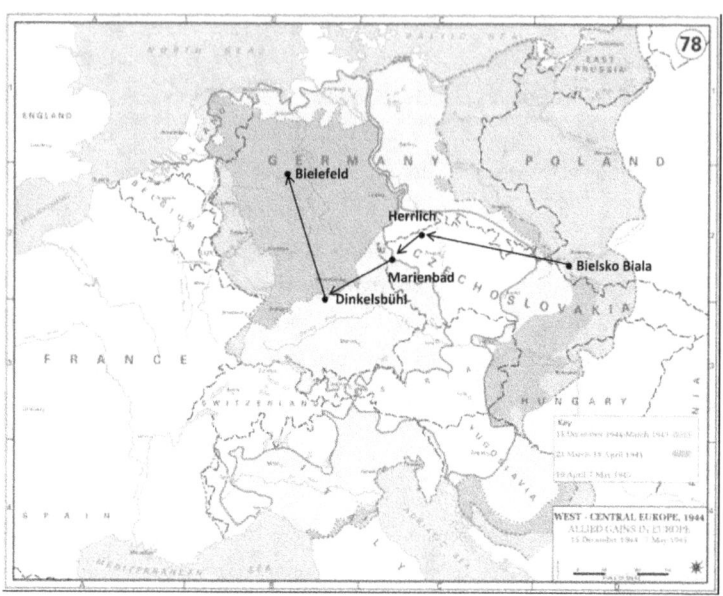

My escape to the west, January 1945–April 1946. (Map courtesy of the Department of History, US Military Academy at West Point. Place names and arrows added by the author.)

called up for action. I was worried that if I told her the truth she might not have let me go, as she felt a sense of responsibility to my mother and family to keep me safe. However, being a committed Nazi, she was supportive of my impending fictional service to the *Vaterland* and helped me get ready to leave. Frau Eckert made an *eiserne Portionen* (iron ration or military ration), for me that consisted of a dozen slices of toasted white bread, a small candle, matches and a small bag of salt, which by that point in the war had been very hard to get. I got my rucksack and put most of the clothes I still had into it. Actually, I didn't have many clothes, as most of what I had was left behind in Bielsko-Biala. I also took a blanket and a spare pair of shoes. I did not take any money as I had no idea if it still had any worth given that the Nazi state had just ceased to exist. In hindsight, I didn't take enough clothes with me and I also, rather foolishly given the circumstances, wore my HJ uniform. Luckily, I got away with it as no one stopped me or arrested me for wearing it. In any case, I had removed all the emblems, epaulettes and other HJ markings.

So, at 6.30 a.m. on 9 May 1945, the HJ members – including my friend Manfred and our HJ leader – left Hrdlovka (Herrlich). Hans didn't come with us as his mother had forbidden it. Hans was needed at home as his father was in the army and his mother had a six-month-old baby to look after. Many years later I found out from Frau Eckert that the road we used to leave was the very road that the Red Army used to enter the village four hours later. It would have been a disaster if we had run into them and I have no idea how we didn't cross paths. Had we run into them, it is very likely we as teenage German boys would have been arrested and sent off to Siberia. Frau Eckert later told me that of all the boys taken by the Soviets only three eventually came back in 1951.

We walked all of that first day together as a group, but the following day we were picked up by two army trucks, which meant the group had to split into two. I ended up on the second truck and before too long the first truck had sped away. We never saw it again. Even before we were split up, we had already lost our HJ leader. Along the way, we heard a fighter aircraft and threw ourselves under cover. After the aircraft left and we picked ourselves up, our leader told us all that we should get rid of what weapons we were carrying: I had been carrying a .22 rifle, and he had a rifle and a *Panzerfaust* anti-tank weapon. He then told us that he was going to go forward by himself to reconnoitre the upcoming territory on his bicycle to see if the Red Army was already there. We never saw him again, though I heard later from Frau Eckert that he eventually managed to escape to the west.

So, by the second day, my group had already been reduced to eight boys on a truck without a leader. Of the eight, only Manfred and I were from Silesia; the rest were Sudeten Germans. We eventually found ourselves in Karlovy Vary[19] (Karlsbad) and I got into an argument with one of the Sudeten Germans, a tall, red-headed 16-year-old boy, who had heard a rumour that US troops were already in the city. We were in the hills overlooking the city and he wanted to leave our truck and go down into the city in search of the Americans even though his evidence that they were there was only a rumour. I thought he was crazy and said so as I thought it was mad to leave our transport in the vain hope that we could find another truck to travel on if the stories weren't true. But I was overruled, and we all left the truck and walked down into the city. Sure enough, there were no US troops there and I swear that if he hadn't been bigger, taller and older than I was, I would have belted him. So we then returned up the hill to where we disembarked our truck to find that it was, unsurprisingly, not there. At this point, my red-headed friend announced that he thought the best option would be for us to turn around and return home. We once again got into an argument as there was no way I was going to walk into the arms of the Red Army, thinking rightly that we were going to be far better off if we made it to the American lines. In the meantime, we had been trying to hitchhike and asked a number of trucks if they could take our group. While a couple of drivers were willing to take one or two, no one had enough space to take all of us.

Eventually it came to a head and the Sudeten Germans decided they would go back, and Manfred said that he would stick with me. Manfred and I had made a deal that our respective families would take each other in depending on what happened: that is, if I found my mother in Bielefeld first, we would take him in, and if Manfred found his family first, then they would take me in. So we said our goodbyes to the Sudeten boys, wished each other luck and, by happy chance, a truck arrived that was able to take both Manfred and me.

But our good luck was short-lived and Manfred and I soon found ourselves hopping from one hitchhiked lift to another. Eventually we found ourselves on a tractor with two guys from the *Reichsarbeitsdienst*[20] (Reich Labour Service). They had a trailer on which were two heavy car engines and a load of special wood chips for modified cars that were fuelled by wood gas.[21] Also on that tractor was a woman from Katowice (Kattowitz) with a son and daughter. Like ourselves, her son was a teenager and the daughter was a couple of years younger. There was also another boy who was travelling alone, and the woman looked after him as best she could. One night, we stopped to sleep and when we woke up the following morning the tractor had left and we were left stuck on the trailer. We spent most of the day watching people and the other refugee traffic go by. The roads were packed full of vehicles of all types and there was an almost endless stream of traffic and humanity all heading west trying to reach the American lines.

Eventually a large Mercedes truck pulled up on the other side of the road. It was owned by on elderly woman from Upper Lusatia (Oberlausitz) in Silesia[22] who had owned a flour mill (Müllenwerke-Stockteich) there; she had filled it up with all her possessions before evacuating. With her were her two daughters, one of whom was about 30 and the other in her mid-40s. The truck had itself been modified to run on the very wood gas that the wood chips in our trailer were designed to produce. So it wasn't too much of a surprise when the driver eventually came over to us and asked if he could have some of the wood chips. Even though the wood chips weren't ours to give, the woman from Katowice (Kattowitz) was shrewd and said, 'Yes, but you have to take us with you.' The driver started to make what to me sounded like excuses about his poor clutch and brakes but when we offered to hook up the trailer and give him all the wood chips we had, he agreed on two conditions: firstly, that we get rid of the two heavy car engines (which were now essentially useless) and secondly, that one person had to stay on the trailer and operate its handbrake during the trip. 'No problem,' said our Kattowitzian friend and we were once again on our way. I didn't quite trust the driver so to make sure he didn't leave us behind, Manfred and I sat rather dangerously on the front bumper bar clutching the guidance poles that were positioned on each side. Manfred and I also rested on the roof of the truck's large wood chip box so that the driver couldn't drive off without us.

In the end, we needn't have bothered. The driver kept his word and allowed us to travel with him until we finally got to the US refugee camp. The Kattowitzian woman rode on the trailer and operated the handbrake as promised while Manfred and I stood ready to use wooden chocks to help stop the truck when required. The trip itself was painfully slow as the roads were packed and it was all stop-start driving. We were lucky to travel three kilometres in a day. One of the strangest things we saw was a group of about 12 Red Army POWs helping an ageing and rather rotund German Luftwaffe soldier towards the American lines. The soldier looked just like the character Sergeant Schultz in the 1960s television comedy series *Hogan's Heroes*. His arms were draped over the shoulders of two Red Army soldiers and they were using their rifles to help support him. It was an unlikely and extraordinary sight.

I don't remember much about what we ate, but food was not easy to come by and you grabbed what you could when you could. On one occasion, Manfred returned from an excursion with two loaves of bread under his arms. He told me that there was a German truck throwing them out to the evacuees and that I should also go and get some. So I went and managed to get a loaf and then waited hoping for a second. I was standing on the rear axle and asked the driver to throw some out from the side of the truck rather than just from the back. He did and I grabbed my second loaf. But just as I did, I could feel someone trying to rip it out from under my arm. I turned round to see a young woman grappling with my bread. It didn't matter what I said to her; she just kept trying to pull it out from under my arm and she seemed to be in some sort of daze. Although I initially hesitated, in the end I struck her on the chest and she fell back onto the ground. Scared that the other people were going to attack me, I ran but it seemed that no one cared, as they themselves were desperate for food. When I got back to the truck, I put both loaves in my rucksack and headed back to see if I could grab another. Sure enough, I once again caught a loaf as it came out of the truck and once again felt someone trying to rip it out from under my arm. I turned round to see an old farmer in his mid-60s trying to grab my bread but this time I did not hesitate to hit him and again make my escape. When I got back to Manfred at the truck, we split up the loaves so that we each had two in case we became separated, and we then shared the fifth.

I only remember eating one warm, cooked meal during that time. One evening we had stopped for the night and one of the two daughters from the Mercedes truck saw me eating a slice of my dry bread. Although we had hardly spoken to each other during the entire trip, she asked me what I was eating, took pity on me and gave me a bowl of warm stew.

Our first sight of the Americans was on the road. Our truck had just stopped in the jammed traffic and on the other side of the road I could see a US jeep slowly driving in our direction. In it was a driver, and in the back were two officers, both of whom were standing up. They all looked confused and disbelieving as they had probably never seen anything like this before: an endless rag-tag column of vehicles full of desperate refugees. I was relieved and said a quiet word of thanks as I thought that the American lines couldn't be far away and that hopefully we were now safe. We soon ended up in a big village and parked on a steep slope only a few hundred metres from a river, and it was that river that was the demarcation line between the US armies and the Red Army. The bridge over the river was guarded by two US Sherman tanks with their guns facing eastwards: that is, in our direction. Just at that moment, five Red Army officers approached with smiles on their faces and we all felt a moment of panic and terror. Some of the women and older men started to cry and I, too, was at the end of my emotional tether. Having done all I could, I now felt that fate held my future in its hands and I just waited to see what would happen. Then a US jeep came towards us with two Americans in it and one asked, 'Why are the people crying?' A woman answered, 'The Russians are here and we are scared of them. We know what they are going to do to us.' The American replied, 'Oh no, this is American-occupied territory and the Russians can't do anything to you – you're safe here.'

I had made it to the American lines.

Thank you, 'Blood and Guts' Patton

It is a quirk of fate that I made it to the safety of US-occupied territory. In fact, the US army shouldn't have been there at all. General George S. Patton, whose nickname was 'Old Blood and Guts', had advanced into the then Czechoslovakia against the intent of the western Allies' agreement with the Soviet Union. Patton didn't like, nor did he trust, the Soviets and would have continued on to liberate and occupy Prague if he had been given the chance but the Supreme Commander of Allied Forces, General Dwight D. Eisenhower, ordered him to stop at the Karlovy Vary-Plzen-Ceska Budejovice line.[23] Nonetheless, Patton had penetrated about 100 kilometres into Czech territory and it was his enthusiasm that allowed me to reach the relative safety of the American lines. Thank you, General Patton.

Despite their alliance against Hitler's Germany, there seemed to me to be no love lost between the US and Soviet forces. Even as we first reached the Americans, there was a very young Red Army soldier who almost got into a very serious confrontation with the Americans. The soldier was in a bad state. He was absolutely filthy, so much so that when beads of sweat ran down his forehead it took some of the dirt with them leaving what almost looked like zebra stripes on his face. He was riding an old German motorbike and in each of his two pockets was a Luger pistol. With him on the back of the bike was a French guy – most likely a liberated slave labourer – and the two of them stole the petrol from the truck directly behind us. The driver, not too impressed, got a US military policeman (MP), who then challenged the Red Army soldier. The soldier was furious and I could see in his face that he would have loved to go for his pistols but they weren't in a convenient position as the barrels rather than the grip and trigger were pointing out of the pockets. The American MP sensed the danger and opened his own side-arm holster ready to draw his weapon should the need arise, and I ducked behind our truck's front axle in case there was any shooting. The MP, huge and grinning as he was, stared down the Red Army soldier who, although fuming, backed off and refilled the truck with the petrol he had tried to steal. After muttering something to his French companion, he rode off with him on the motorbike and never returned.

The Red Army soldiers were generally in very poor shape. They were hungry and dirty, and their uniforms and equipment looked used and in bad condition. Their wounded were being transported on horse-drawn carts that had been covered in straw and the whole impression was that of an army that was not well-provisioned or supported. On one occasion, a car with a female soldier standing on its sideboard stopped as one of our group was slicing off a chunk of bread. She stuck out her hand, wanting some. We didn't give her any and she drove off but for a while I was worried she'd come back with some of her comrades at night and give us a hard time. Thankfully they didn't. I also managed to get my wristwatch taken by a Red Army soldier. It wasn't a very good watch as it kept stopping and had to be wound regularly. When the soldier initially took it, it wasn't working, so he gave it back. Foolishly, I wound it up and when he heard it ticking took it off me again and offered a few cigarettes as compensation. I swore at him in German which, thankfully, he didn't understand and although I could have reported it to the Americans I didn't think it was worth the trouble.

On a lighter note, I'll never forget a Red Army officer who had managed to procure a bicycle for himself. It, too, was in bad condition as it had no rubber tyres on the rims, but it didn't matter to him: he was proud as punch as he rode it along the road with a big smile on his face.

Life in the refugee camp

Even though we were so close to the bridge, the Americans told us that we'd have to take a detour to reach the refugee camp which they themselves called a displaced persons or DPs camp. So, we backed up and turned down a side road but the Mercedes truck was starting to falter and needed a bit of attention. After clearing the radiator and refilling it with water from a nearby lake, we were again able to get underway. The camp itself was just outside of Mariánské Lázne (Marienbad). The city was only 10 kilometres from the Czech-German border and, like Karlovy Vary (Karlsbad), was also a historic spa town. Run by the US army, the camp was on a former Luftwaffe auxiliary airfield which had been ploughed over so that it could no longer be used to operate aircraft. It had what looked like a concrete bunker, on top of which was a huge radar dish.[24]

Actually, if I had known then that I was so close to the border, I would have taken off by myself during the night. In any case, we weren't in the camp for very long, only about three weeks. When we first got there, Manfred came upon the idea of swapping our HJ daggers for cigarettes. Apart from smoking, cigarettes were also good for use as barter for other goods. We approached one of the 18-year-old guards and asked if he wanted one. He agreed to a swap of one dagger for one packet of Camels: my first American cigarettes.

We received no food during the first three days and I began snooping around the camp for whatever I could find. There were a few smashed barracks so I thought I would take a look. In the rubble of one of the buildings, I found, in a small ornamental table, a partially cut loaf of bread. I sliced off a piece and, not wanting to be greedy, left the area and watched to see if anyone else turned up. No one did, but had they done so I would have asked before I took any more. My restraint did me no good as the following day I returned, but someone else had taken the remaining loaf. So, I kept looking and eventually found a 5x8-centimetre piece of smoked bacon rind. Even back in Bielsko-Biala, I used to love eating bacon rind. For me it was a sort of chewing gum, so I took the rind, cut it into spoon-sized pieces and heated it using a spoon that I had also found as well as the matches and candle that Frau Eckert had given me. Given my hunger and the circumstances, it tasted quite good.

The camp was supplied with water through some pipes that had been compromised by a shell or bomb hit and we were warned not to drink the water unless it had been boiled. By the third day, I got dysentery because I had drunk the contaminated water, which was a real problem, as the Americans had begun to distribute food. Manfred brought me freshly baked bread that was still hot to touch but I couldn't eat any of it. In the end, I gave all my rations to Manfred. For the next three days, I was lying on the trailer covered with a tarpaulin. I felt weak and eventually I couldn't cope any more so I went down to the camp's first did station, which was being run by members of the German army's Red Cross unit, and asked for help. Just as they were explaining that they were on their lunch break, I began to pass out. They took me inside and gave me an orally ingested dose of morphine which I remember being unbelievably bitter. They then repeated the treatment for the next two days. So, by the time I had recovered, I had gone without food for about six days.

Slowly our rations increased. Our first cooked meals were a modest amount – about 300 grams – of potatoes and green peas with a sort of potato flour sauce mixture on top of it, but with no meat or butter. At first, food was only served at lunchtime, but then we eventually also got two slices of bread for breakfast. In the end, we settled into a routine of bread for breakfast with the potatoes and peas mix for lunch, then on the following day we received soup for lunch and two slices of bread in the evening. Then the cycle repeated. The only meat we ate was when Manfred and I stole some preserved goose meat from the Mercedes truck on which we had been travelling. Having not had meat for so long, we found it unbelievably delicious and we then bartered the left-over gravy in the jars for about 500 grams of sugar.

Despite it being run by the US army, the camp had a German *Kommandant* who also happened to come from Silesia. The *Kommandant* was subordinate to the US camp commander and was in charge of the camp's bureaucracy. All the DPs in the camp had to report him and give their details. Apart from the Germans, there were many other nationalities including Russians, Hungarians, Romanians and Poles. As we reported to the *Kommandant*, he offered us extra rations to do some extra work for him. So, we became his personal helpers but our reward was some poorly prepared and usually burnt soup made from the camp's stale bread. Once we stumbled across some dehydrated spreadable cheese that had fallen on the floor and while he offered it to us as part of our 'extra rations', I felt that we were getting taken advantage of and I 'resigned' as his helper. A threat by the *Kommandant* to tell the US camp commander didn't mean anything to me, as I was sure the US commander was far too busy to occupy himself with our petty disputes.

I was wrong. Not too long after, I heard a sort of scratching sound on the side of the tent Manfred and I were sleeping in. The 'scratch' was, in fact, the 'knock' of the US camp commander and he asked in broken German if he could enter. I said. 'Of course: you are the commander and you can do whatever you like.' Very politely he said, 'No, I can't. This is your tent – your personal space – and I will only come in if I have your permission.' I was flabbergasted. This was something I certainly wasn't used to, having grown up with adults constantly telling me what to do with very little consideration of what I thought. I invited him in and he then asked about the situation with the *Kommandant*. At the same time, he also explained that he was in the process of improving the camp by digging latrines, cleaning up rubbish and generally organising it so that it was as functional and hospitable as it could be. To do that, he said, he needed people who were able to work to join in and the *Kommandant* had said that I wasn't willing to work. I very quickly corrected him, saying, 'I'm very happy to do my share of the work, but we were promised extra rations by the *Kommandant* and he hasn't kept his part of the deal. I won't be taken advantage of.' The US camp commander offered a double ration to all those who worked. I told him I was sceptical given everything I had already experienced, but he gave his word that if I didn't get my double ration I could walk into his office anytime and he would personally make sure I got it. I was impressed and agreed to work the following day. It wasn't really work. To me it seemed more like 'busy work' to make sure we weren't bored. The irony was, when Manfred and I got our second rations, we were unable to eat them all in one go. We were so used to the meagre food we had been eating over the previous weeks that our stomachs had shrunk. It didn't go to waste, though. We just ate it in small portions spread out during the day.

The Americans actually treated us well and, given the circumstances, I find it hard to fault them. For example, there was a story that went around the camp which I heard so often from so many people that it was almost certainly true. A group of local Czechs were making money for themselves by trading and selling goods such as rations coupons in the local town. One day, having heard some women speaking German during their excursion to the town, they became suspicious of who they were and followed them back into the camp. One of them then confronted a decorated German army sergeant; they wanted to take his medals and other military decorations – presumably so that they could sell them. An American MP challenged him and put his pistol to the guy's forehead saying, 'This soldier has earned his medals through service to his country and you are not going to take them from him!' While I doubt the MP would ever have pulled the trigger, the threat was more than enough to send the Czech packing. After that, none of the local Czechs ever entered the camp again.

The only inappropriate thing that the Americans did was that, one day, there was a call over the loudspeakers saying, 'Due to espionage, all cameras, radios and binoculars are to be surrendered to the camp authorities.' Dutifully, we all surrendered the relevant items. It didn't bother us too much as we were still grateful to have reached the American lines and generally felt ourselves lucky. Over the next few days, however, it became apparent that the Americans were walking around the camp with all our surrendered goods: they had effectively stolen them.

In the camp were also German prisoners of war (POWs). They were separated from us and placed in a set of barracks across the road, which was guarded by the Americans with watch-towers and machine guns. Manfred and I befriended one of them, a young 18-year-old called Heinz. One morning we saw the POWs assembled and they were given some news which caused a very angry response and a sort of collective 'growl' could be heard. My impression at the time was that they were going to be handed over to the Red Army, and that is what caused the 'disturbance'.

What I didn't know then was that there was almost certainly a young Günter Grass at that camp at the same time I was. Although I never met him, Günter Grass was then a 17-year-old POW after having been wounded on 20 April 1945 and then captured by the US. He had been placed in the Marienbad DP/POW camp in early May 1945.[25] Eventually, Grass was transferred by the Americans, along with other German POWs, to the western zone of occupation and ultimately released in April 1946. So, perhaps none or not all of the German POWs at the Marienbad DP camp were handed over to the Soviet Union and, even though I never heard from him again, perhaps Heinz also made it to the west.

Although a 'nobody' at the time, Grass went on to become one of Germany's leading post-war left-wing intellectuals, writing famous novels such as *Die Blechtrommel* (*The Tin Drum*), which was also made into a movie in 1979. In 1999, he won the Nobel Prize for literature. Grass had been a member of the Waffen SS – a fact he only controversially admitted to in 2006, just before publication of his memoir *Beim Häuten der Zwiebel* (*Peeling the Onion*). Some thought that this undercut his moral authority as he had previously claimed that he had been drafted into an air defence unit in 1944.[26] Grass remains a controversial figure, having criticised Israel with a poem, '*Was gesagt werden muss*' ('What must be said'), in 2012.

Suddenly after three weeks in the camp, we were told by the Americans one evening to get ourselves ready as we were going to be transferred from the camp into Germany the following morning. We were all very happy to hear that. To us, the most important thing was to get to Germany. For me, the travails of past few weeks had all been worth it.

Lucky for some, unlucky for others

To someone living in Australia, Germany or other peaceful Western country in the 21st century, the events I experienced in the six months from January to June 1945 probably seem quite harrowing, and indeed they were. As a 14-year-old boy, I suddenly had to look after myself under circumstances which even grown adults found confronting and challenging. In a sense, it made a 'man' out of me. I was, however, quite lucky compared to others. Despite the hardships, I was uninjured and I had not suffered any violence, abuse or incarceration. Above all, I had escaped the Soviets and made it to the West, where I eventually had the chance to live my life in a prosperous, free and democratic society. Others weren't so lucky.

My experience as a refugee is a small part of a much greater story about the flight and forced removal or ethnic cleansing of Germans and ethnic Germans from eastern Europe after World War II. Largely unknown outside of Germany, between 10 and 14 million Germans were uprooted and sent west. This is not only the largest forced migration in history but probably the largest single movement of population in history.[27] There were many, like me, who fled west of their own accord when the Red Army came through, fearful of the consequences of being in their path and not wanting to live under Soviet rule. In July 1945, the Big Three – Soviet leader Josef Stalin, US President Truman and the UK's prime ministers Churchill and Atlee[28] – met at the Potsdam Conference. There, the borders of post-war Europe were redrawn and Germany ceded nearly 30 per cent of its pre-1938 territory, leaving large ethnic German minorities as new constituents of Czechoslovakia and Poland. The Soviet Union and the newly-independent eastern European communist states also included large ethnic German populations that had lived there for centuries[29] – in the case of the Baltic States, for over 800 years. The governments of Poland, Czechoslovakia, Yugoslavia, and the Soviet Union considered all these German civilian populations 'dangerous' despite their diverse political ideologies, and nearly the entirety of the German population were force marched into labour camps or into a post-war Germany that their ancestors had not seen for centuries. Although the Potsdam agreement stipulated that their removal was supposed to be 'orderly and humane', the reality was very different.

Before the Potsdam Conference were the 'wild expulsions' where the local authorities removed the local populations. They were not 'wild', as they were organised, and the police, troops and militias who carried them out were acting under orders and more often than not acting under direction of the highest authorities.[30] Finally, the better organised and systematic expulsions occurred after the Potsdam Conference. This included those expulsions undertaken, for example, under the Beneš Decrees in Czechoslovakia.[31] In total, approximately 500,000 expellees died during the expulsions due to hypothermia, starvation and, to a lesser extent, direct violence. The Red Cross and the Federal Republic of Germany's government cite a less demonstrable figure of 2.2 million deaths.[32]

My future wife, whom I was to meet in Bielefeld, was also an expellee from Silesia along with her family. In April 1946 the new Polish authorities knocked on their door in their small village near Wroclaw (Breslau) and gave them only a short time to leave. My mother-in-law, who was a proud woman, finished washing her dishes and put a small vase with a flower in it on the table for the new Polish owners. They then left with whatever they could carry and made their way to the train station, where they boarded trains headed west into occupied Germany.

Some famous names can trace part of their family history to these events. In the Federal Republic of Germany, Joschka Fischer, foreign minister in the government led by Gerhard Schröder (1998–2005), was from a family of ethnic Germans who were expelled from Hungary.[33] In Australia, the comedian Adam Hills, who for many years hosted the hit music show *Spicks & Specks*, can trace his ancestry back to Sudeten Germans who were also expelled from Czechoslovakia after the war. As part of the television series, *Who Do You Think You Are?*,[34] Adam traced his family back to a small village near the German-Czech border called Hora Svatého Šebestiána (Sankt Sebastiansberg) and he met his relatives who are now living in Germany. When he returned to the village, all traces of its German history had been removed. Incidentally, Hora Svatého Šebestiána (Sankt Sebastiansberg) is only about 50 kilometres from Hrdlovka (Herrlich).

Although my mother and I made it to the west, my sister Irene and my great aunt Antonina did not. They remained in Hrdlovka (Herrlich) when I left. Frau Eckert later told me that, despite everything, the Red Army was well-behaved when they reached Hrdlovka (Herrlich) and once there, they told all the evacuees to go back to the home towns. There was, however, no transport and Antonina and my sister started to walk back using the railway-tracks as a guide. But given that my auntie was about 70 years old, and my sister was about 10 years old, travelling by foot was very arduous and they didn't get very far. Eventually they took shelter in a nunnery. There, during the night, Antonina began to scream and shout. She made an awful noise and then suddenly fell silent. The following morning she was found dead – presumably from a heart attack. My sister Irene was eventually sent by the authorities to her grandmother's house. There, she was treated very poorly and the local people eventually signed a petition to have her removed and placed in the care of another family. Irene stayed in what became Communist Czechoslovakia, settling in the town then known as Gottwaldov; it has since been renamed Zlín.

My foster family, concerned that the local Czechs were about to take revenge on them as Nazis, left Czechoslovakia of their own accord before the expulsions and settled in what was to become Communist East Germany. But that was not before Herr Eckert, our courageous Nazi stormtrooper, tried to kill himself by jumping into the local lake. Luckily for him, he was rescued before he drowned.

Despite my ordeal, I was grateful that I had come out of it alive, safe and uninjured. But life in post-war Germany was not going to be easy. Far from it.

Four

Post-war Germany

The morning after we were ordered by the Americans to prepare for our departure – 7 June 1945 – about 20 US army trucks arrived in the camp. We were told to take only what we could carry, and we were then loaded up with 20 people per truck. The trucks, though, also had a trailer, so it was possible for us to take a reasonable amount of personal belongings. Manfred and I broke down our tent and he took half and I took the other half.

One of the US soldiers, who was of German descent (he spoke German) and who was a bit mean-spirited, was going from truck to truck taking people's personal items and throwing them to the ground. In one of the trucks in front of us there was an elderly couple who had their bedding with them, which he also threw to the ground. As soon as the soldier moved on, the elderly man, quick as a flash, jumped down and picked up the bedding and threw it back on board. The other US soldiers burst out laughing, taking pleasure in the spectacle of seeing their comrade being embarrassed. When we finally got under way, all we knew was that we were being taken into Germany. We had no idea about our final destination.

'Die Stunde Null'

The Germany into which we were travelling was a desolate and desperate place. Not only was Germany militarily defeated; its cities and industry were devastated by Allied air raids, and large portions of the population were suffering from hunger and the loss of their homes. Moreover, it was occupied and divided by the four victorious powers and morally bankrupt as a result of the Holocaust and other Nazi crimes. In Germany today, the end of World War II is referred to as *Die Stunde Null* – the Zero Hour – a point of time at which everything begins again.

Germany had been divided into four occupation zones. The Soviet Union had the eastern provinces such as Brandenburg, Thuringia and Saxony. In the west, the British governed the north, which included Hamburg and the devastated cities of the Ruhr Valley; the French governed the far west of the country around the Rhine River; and the US controlled the southern sector, particularly the region of Bavaria, which included the German portion of the European Alps. The running joke was 'The Americans got the scenery, the French got the wine and the British got the ruins.' The capital Berlin, too, was divided along similar lines.[1]

US President Truman issued a directive to General Eisenhower on 17 October 1945 through which the US occupation zone was administered. Part of that directive laid down the governance arrangements between the four commanders-in-chief of the occupying powers. Together, they constituted the Allied Control Council (ACC), which was the supreme authority of control over Germany.[2] A further part of Truman's directive included the goal of 'demilitarisation': that is, all German armed forces were to be dissolved. Furthermore, Germany's industrial capacity to make war was also to be eliminated. In a ruling specifically relating to the IG Farben conglomerate,[3] the ACC stated that its broader goal was 'to ensure that Germany will never again threaten her neighbours or the peace of the world'.[4] I myself remember hearing General Eisenhower on the radio saying that 'no German shall ever again bear arms'. And nobody was happier to hear that than the Germans themselves.

Road trip and arrival

Although the ride itself was uneventful, the journey was not. The trucks themselves were without tarpaulins and open to the weather. Although Manfred had found a comfortable space to sit, I was sitting on the tailgate, which pretty soon became uncomfortable, and I eventually squeezed into a spot next to him. We travelled all day and, on the way, we passed a number of US army trucks travelling in the opposite direction, most of which were carrying east Europeans who had been forced into slave labour. Nazi

Germany's war economy had been supported by millions of slave labourers who had been forcibly deported and made to work in the Third Reich so as to release manpower for the Wehrmacht and the arms industries.[5] Now, with the war over, they were being repatriated to their homelands. At one stage we also passed through Nuremberg. Nuremberg had been a large city, and home to the yearly Nazi Party rallies as documented by Leni Riefenstahl's *Triumph of the Will*. For kilometre after kilometre, there was nothing to see but burnt-out and blasted ruins as the city had been utterly destroyed by Allied bombing raids and the street battles during April 1945 through which the Allies had taken the city.

In the evening we arrived in, as it turned out, Dinkelsbühl, a medieval town in southern Germany which was then part of the US occupation zone. Dinkelsbühl is associated with cultural romanticism and was completely undamaged during the war.[6] Today, its historic old town is perfectly preserved and one of Europe's most important cultural monuments.[7] But cultural history and architectural beauty were not on my mind when we arrived. The Americans unceremoniously dumped us in the city's central square and left immediately. There were many people standing in groups so, not sure what to do, I went from one group to another asking what was happening. Much to my surprise, almost everyone self-identified according to their province: that is, they would answer 'I'm a Saxon' or 'I'm a Thüringien'. When I came across a group of Austrians and I identified myself as German, they got very angry and told me to 'get lost'.

Eventually, I met a farmer with a cart who explained that the foreign slave labour was gone and they needed people to help with the upcoming harvest. He offered to take me in. At that point I had an interest in becoming a farmer, so I agreed. As there was very little transport, most people simply dumped the goods they had brought but could not carry in Dinkelsbühl's central square, and either walked or took basic transport to their accommodation. The three elderly women with whom I had travelled on the Mercedes truck travelled on the same cart as I did, but many people simply ended up walking the nine kilometres to the village. The truck itself had been left in the DP camp along with all the other vehicles as a form of war reparation to the Czechs. Manfred was initially taken in by the *Burgermeister* (town mayor).

Down on the farm

When we arrived at the village of Obermichelbach, the local farmers were already waiting for us. I don't know how the arrangements had been made, but we as refugees were allocated to various people around the village for somewhere to live and work. Even those who couldn't work – for example, the three elderly women from the Mercedes truck – were also given lodgings. The three women, unlike the rest of us, did have some money so perhaps it wasn't as big a burden on their host as it was with the rest of us.

I eventually spent 10 months in that village but living there killed off whatever enthusiasm I ever had for being a farmer. Farming was extremely hard work – between 12 and 14 hours a day in summer – and village life generally was terribly boring, as there was absolutely no entertainment to enjoy when one wasn't working. The farmers themselves were extremely difficult to understand, with their thick Bavarian accents, and they also treated us very poorly. The farmers generally, and my farmer in particular, didn't seem to realise that most of us were from the cities and knew virtually nothing about farming and, in my case, I was only 14 years old. We were also fresh out of a refugee camp and had only been given basic

St Michael's Church in the village of Obermichelbach where I lived from June 1945 to April 1946. (Andrew Gaczol)

rations to survive on. When we had our first meals together, I told the farmer that I wasn't used to the thick, rich food they were serving. Having been in the DP camp and before that on the run from the Red Army, the milk, meat and other foods they were offering were difficult for me to digest. After a few days, I fell sick with colic. For three days, I was in extreme pain but I got very little sympathy from my farmer as he thought I was just trying to avoid working.

Slowly I got better but, having had the farmer give me a hard time just for being sick, I went to the village mayor and asked to be relocated. He obliged. I was moved to a new farm and for a few weeks I was treated better. But after that, I started to get treated poorly once more and the farmer and I had a number of arguments. On one occasion, an 18-year-old former soldier, who had also been taken in by the farmer, and I were sitting in our room and I explained to him that I thought we weren't being treated very well and that I had little regard for our farmer host. Unbeknown to me, he was standing directly outside and had heard everything. He stormed in with the rest of his family and gave me a beating.

On another occasion, he threw a pitchfork of manure on me. I was very angry and told him that I was no longer going to work that day. Although at that age I had very little idea about democracy and workers' rights, I explained that I was on strike. When I returned to the farmhouse, the farmer's wife was also very unhappy with me as ultimately it was she who would have to do the work if I kept having arguments with her husband. I did feel bad about this, as she already had a lot of work to do herself. I never did get on with him, and on one occasion he threatened to run me through with a pitchfork, and I in turn threatened the same. It seemed to me that, having become used to ordering around their foreign slave labourers, the farmers thought that they could treat displaced Germans, such as me, the same. Eventually I was given a miserly 150 Reichsmarks for 10 months' work, but I never got paid a regular wage and he never replaced the clothes that got ruined while I was working for him.

As for Manfred, he was eventually placed on a farm across the road and, although he was worked for longer hours, he seemed to cope better than I did. Manfred's farmer had also promised him a new suit and shoes as a Christmas gift and that kept him motivated, but it also meant he lost his enthusiasm to keep travelling with me until I reached Bielefeld. In the end, the farmer went back on his word and Manfred got nothing. He too had been taken advantage of.

Mother and son

It was in February 1946 that I re-established contact with my mother. One evening, I got a message from the village *Burgermeister* that a letter from my mother had arrived. I was having dinner but I dropped everything and ran in my socks (there was still snow and ice on the ground at that time) to the *Burgermeister*'s house and got the letter. Letters at that point were quite something as war damage meant that mail took four weeks to arrive due to the country's smashed roads and bridges. I took the letter home, read it and was very upset to find out that my mother had already written me only to have the letter returned to her. She knew where I was as I had already written to her in Bielefeld, but her first attempt to reply had been sent back with the phrase 'Addressed to person unknown'. I was furious. The next day I went to the postman and told him off so severely that he just stood there cowering. He didn't even try to defend himself.

I wrote back to my mother and told her I wasn't very happy in Bavaria living a farmer's life and wanted to be reunited with her as quickly as possible. My mother asked what sort of work I was interested in so that she could see if there were any apprenticeship positions available. I told her I wanted to be a motor mechanic and she agreed that I could come up to Bielefeld. But, strangely, she insisted that I keep her agreement for me to come a secret and that, if asked, I was to say I came to Bielefeld of my own accord without my mother's knowledge. The impression I had was that, in this way, my mother could plead ignorance if my arrival caused any problems with her landlord.

Despite our initial deal, Manfred and I fell out a bit and, in the end, he didn't follow me to Bielefeld when I finally made contact with my mother. I was already a little frustrated with him as he always seemed to rely on me to organise things; we had an argument after he was, in my opinion, unforgivably rude to one of the local farm girls. From then on, we stayed distant from each other and no longer met up to just talk and hang out. When he found out that I was leaving, he was suddenly very forthcoming and asked why I hadn't been speaking with him and letting me know what was happening. I didn't really respond. We eventually said our goodbyes and I didn't see him again. I heard later that he was reunited with his family in October 1946 and he ended up in what became East Germany.

So, at the end of April 1946, I got my things together, such as clothes and my various ration coupons, and checked out of the local *Burgeramt* (Residents Registration Office), which in this case was the *Burgermeister*'s office. The daughter of the elderly lady from the Mercedes truck generously gave me a set of lady's skiing trousers (which might sound a bit strange but I didn't care as I had no long trousers at all) and a leather hunting bag, and the farmer's wife gave me a four-kilogram loaf of bread and 20 eggs. According to an old superstition, she cut off the first slice of bread, as to do otherwise meant bad luck. The *Burgermeister* offered to take me to the railway station, but I took the bus. I was, however, very grateful for the offer as the *Burgermeister* was a busy man and had other tasks to be going on with. I thanked him sincerely as he had been as helpful as anyone could have expected him to be during my stay. From there, I went up to the main street and caught the bus to the main train station in Dinkelsbühl.

At the time, one couldn't book a ticket directly to one's destination if that destination was over a long distance. Like the mail, personal transport was dependent on how much war damage existed on the roads, bridges and railway lines between you and your journey's end. So, in the first instance, I could only book a ticket to Nuremberg. Having bought my ticket, by chance I ran into a family who had also been in the Marienbad refugee camp. The woman and two boys, one of whom was called Wolfgang, had been in the truck next to ours while we had been on the road in the Sudetenland. So, we kept each other company on the train journey from Dinkelsbühl to Nuremberg. Also part of the group was a guy called Walter who was originally from Nuremberg and whom I had met in the village near Dinkelsbühl.

Judgement at Nuremberg

I had first visited Nuremberg in February 1946 after I made a brief excursion to the Soviet occupation zone with Manfred and the elderly

Hauptbahnhof (main train station), Nuremberg, where I was effectively arrested. Photo taken in 2005. (Andrew Gaczol)

woman who owned the Mercedes truck. Walter had already invited Manfred and me to visit him and his family in Nuremberg should the opportunity ever present itself, so we did. I spent three or four days there, looked around the historic medieval castle and what was left of the city. Walter's family were generous in their hospitality and also provided us with meals.

On this occasion in April 1946, my travel companions and I arrived in Nuremberg in the evening, and it was then that I said farewell to Walter for the last time, as he then returned to live with his family. Tired and hungry, the rest of us thought we would see if we could find a meal or hot tea at the local Red Cross. Halfway to the Red Cross station – which wasn't far from the main Nuremberg train station – we were stopped by a US army lieutenant and a German civilian in a trench coat. They asked Wolfgang to go with them. He wasn't keen to join them but rather stupidly I encouraged him as my previous experience with the Americans had been that if you helped them out they would give you some form of reward, like chocolate or cigarettes. I then followed the three of them, hoping to also pick up some goods. What I hadn't initially noticed was that there were two US army trucks and two jeeps parked just outside the train station. The two jeeps were each armed with a mounted machine

Palace of Justice, Nuremberg, behind which I was held in custody and where the International Military Tribunal held trials of Nazi leaders. Photo taken in 2005. (Andrew Gaczol)

gun and they bookended the two trucks. Although I tried to disengage myself at that point, it was too late and the German in the trench coat insisted I remain with them. We were put on one of the US army trucks, which was already full with some young men who looked a bit rough to me. From there we were taken to the Nuremberg Palace of Justice, which was the very same building where the International Military Tribunal was then conducting the war crimes trials against the Nazi leadership.

We were taken the sub-regional office for the US Counter Intelligence Corps (CIC) which was within the compound behind the Palace of Justice. At first we were interrogated individually. This included being stripped naked to see if we had any tattoos that might have indicted SS membership.[8] Our clothes were also searched.

We were then taken to a large hall where a pot-bellied US major was sitting behind a desk. There we waited and, after having a disagreement with one of the other captives, I was told off in Czech by a US army lieutenant who, it seemed to me, had been left in the room to listen to our conversations. At one stage, two tall slim chaps marched into the room in unison, presented themselves to the US major and then identified themselves as former SS officers. They were asked by the US major if they had been in a POW camp, and whether they had their discharge papers. On each occasion they answered 'Yes' in military unison, and then eventually marched out in unison, not looking either left or right as if they were still on a military parade ground. It was quite remarkable and impressive in its own way. Despite defeat and capture, it appeared that they were not apprehensive or intimidated at all.

We were eventually put back on the US army trucks and transferred to a gaol where we spent four days. We had mugshot photos taken of us complete with numbers, and our fingerprints were taken as well. We also got very little food with only oats for breakfast and dry bread. I was furious to the point of tears that I had been arrested and put in gaol without having done anything and made a little protest by deliberately smearing my fingerprints. The US officer taking my prints said, 'Well, that's a nice set of fingerprints!' but he didn't make me do them again. Although I didn't know it at the time, Wolfgang's parents had tried to find a lawyer to get our release but the Americans wouldn't allow it.

On the second day, a guy was put in our cell early in the morning. It was made to look as if he had been picked up like we had been at the train station. But the strange thing was that he was wearing a US army olive-green tank-top shirt. This was unusual because normally anyone wearing US clothing had it immediately repossessed by the Americans regardless of the circumstances – even if it meant they were left half-naked. Unlike the US army lieutenant who might have been in the large hall for other reasons, I was definitely convinced that this guy was a plant to pass information on us back to the Americans. He would try to make lots of conversation and every so often he would be taken from the cell only to return a few hours later. So, I said the bare minimum.

Wolfgang and I were finally released on the fourth day and we were told to leave Nuremberg within 12 hours otherwise we'd be locked up again, but this time for six weeks. As it was nine a.m. and my train wasn't until one a.m. the following day – more than 12 hours – this left me with a problem. Both Wolfgang and I then went back to an apartment, where we essentially hid until we could get the early morning train. On the way there, we had been very careful to check around corners to avoid any Americans. Thankfully his family had kept my rucksack with my food and other belongings in it and I was able to retrieve it before I left for Bielefeld.

Although I eventually got on the train and was able to continue my journey, I never did find out why I was detained. Perhaps the US authorities were still chasing people who they suspected of being Werewolves or perhaps it was because they thought I might be associated with the *Edelweißpiraten* (Edelweiss Pirates), who had been reported attacking Polish and Russian refugees and German women who had been fraternising with the US or British occupation soldiers.[9] Again, I was comparatively lucky, apart from the annoyance of a time delay I suffered no harm. Others housed in the Palace of Justice met a different fate.

On my way again

The remaining train trip took a few days. Although I can't remember exactly how long, it was at least two nights, with one of them spent in a concrete air raid bunker. At one point, while waiting at a train station, I cut off a slice of my bread and began to eat it. An ex-soldier was on the train platform, as was a civilian with his 10-year-old daughter. Food was short everywhere and, selfish as it may sound today, I didn't really want to share my bread as it was all I had to eat during the coming few days of travel. I was already short as Wolfgang had, without asking, relieved me of some of it when we were first released from gaol. The ex-soldier said, 'Could you at least give the young girl a slice?', so I did. But then everyone expected a piece and they got upset at me when I didn't oblige. It was either that, or I was going to be the one going hungry well before I reached my destination. Clothes were also in short supply, and I was advised that while sleeping I should place my shoes with the legs of my cot in them or otherwise they would almost certainly be stolen during the night. In the end I slept in my shoes, just to be sure, and Wolfgang and I took turns sleeping; that way, at least one of us was always awake, so our things wouldn't get stolen.

Bielefeld

Wolfgang and I parted company when we arrived at Bielefeld as his village was a bit further along the rail line. I had arrived mid-morning – at about 10 o'clock – and I started asking people for directions to the trams. My

Bielefeld seen from the top of the Sparrenburg Castle. Photo taken in 2013. (Andrew Gaczol)

mother had given me a written set of instructions on how to get to her home and I eventually caught the correct tram and found my way there.

The landlady asked me who I was, so I gave her my name and told her I was looking for my mother. 'Oh, you silly boy,' she began, 'why didn't you stay on the farm? At least you had food there. We don't have anything here.' She went on and on and then asked, 'Can you take your clothes off and wash? You smell like the farm.' I must admit, I did smell pretty rank, having travelled for three or four days and been held in captivity for four more. I never had the opportunity to wash either myself or my clothes and I must have been quite on the nose. A widow, the landlady offered me a jacket from her dead husband which I gratefully accepted even though it was a bit too big. She then offered to walk me to the factory where my mother worked, which I also gratefully accepted. It was a 15-minute walk and I was very excited as we arrived at the gatehouse – it had been 15 months and I was so happy to be seeing my mother again. The gatekeeper called her and she came out. I was on the verge of tears and gave her a huge hug. With an emotional outburst that would have brought the house down, she simply responded, '*So, da bist du ja schon wieder…* (So, here you are again…)' She then explained that I would have to wait until work was over at five p.m. before she could come home and we could meet up again and talk.

Bielefeld today is a city of about 320,000 people in the state of Nord

Bielenfeld Altstadt as it is today. (Andrew Gaczol)

Rhein Westphalen. Once the centre of a thriving textile industry, the city celebrated its 800th anniversary during 2014. It also holds the rather dubious honour of being considered one of Germany's most boring cities – so much so that recently an internet meme known as the Bielefeld Conspiracy has evolved that claims that the city is so boring it doesn't actually exist.

But the Bielefeld of 1946 was very different. Then, it had only about 130,000 people. On 30 September 1944, the old historic city centre – the Altstadt – was all but destroyed during an air raid which killed hundreds. My mother was almost killed during 1945 when, during an air raid, she was saved by a Dutch forced labourer when a wall collapsed at the Anker-Werke AG factory. Perhaps this was 'karma' as she had previously been giving him extra food from the canteen. In March 1945, the Royal Air Force's famous 617 Squadron, the Dam Busters, successfully targeted the city's railway viaduct with specially designed ten-ton 'Grand Slam' bombs.[10] I myself saw the viaduct ruin after I arrived. Surrounding the ruin for one square kilometre there was nothing but bomb craters.[11] In April 1945, the US army took the city and, after the German surrender on 8 May, it was handed over to the British occupation authorities.[12]

In the Altstadt, there were narrow laneways that had been cleared between the rubble so that people could move through the city. Rubble clearance, with small locomotives, started quite early. In Bielefeld, as in all German cities, groups of women gathered to help clear the rubble and to salvage as many usable bricks as possible. The practice was dominated by women as most of the young and able men had been killed during the war[13] and eventually the phenomenon became known as *die Trümmerfrauen* (the rubble women).[14] The rubble was so bad that as late as 1947, the Bielefeld city council compulsorily conscripted all available able-bodied men for three days to help clear the city of rubble and rubbish.

Having spent 10 months in the US occupation zone, I found it an interesting contrast to observe the British soldiers in Bielefeld. While the American soldiers were reasonably generous to children and gave them chewing gum and chocolate, the British soldiers weren't as charitable, as they were less generously provisioned by their own government. For example, while a US soldier might offer you a cigarette, the British soldier was likely to ask you for one. The UK soldiers were less well liked than the American soldiers. They were not hated, but you couldn't engage with them easily, whereas the US soldiers were generally more affable and approachable.

The building in which my mother and I lived was also undergoing some repair work so I decided to help where I could, partly because salvaging and rebuilding seemed to the right thing to do, but also because I was hoping that I would be rewarded for my work with either food or with goods that I could barter on the black market. So I toiled hard clearing rubble, salvaging bricks and making cement. For all my efforts I eventually received a pear! One pear. I was furious. I was then asked to help out on the building opposite us and I refused. They then asked my mother to allow me to help them. Even though I explained what had happened, she encouraged me to go, so I did, trusting their assurances that this time would be different. The result was exactly the same: I worked very hard and was given virtually nothing. This time I got a handful of tiny pears, each of which was barely a bite. Third time unlucky, I was asked through my mother by a neighbouring baker to help with his rebuilding. Although we negotiated a payment of a loaf of bread, the loaf I eventually got was only two-thirds the size of a standard loaf. But at least it was better than the previous pair of rip-offs.

All this wasn't much of a surprise as, like many immigrants, we were given a hard time by the local people. In a classic case of blame the victim, the local West Germans said things like 'You're foreigners – what are you doing here?'; 'You're taking our jobs'; 'Why don't you go back to where you came from?'; 'You must have done something wrong to have been on the run'; and so on. The same happens in Australia and elsewhere today with immigrants and those who seek asylum. Some things don't seem to change.

The landlady herself, despite a poor first impression, was actually a friendly and warm-hearted person and she helped me where she could. For instance, she would sometimes prepare food for me while I was away at work and leave it for me in my room upon my return. She also helped me get odd jobs with various people so I could earn a little extra money or some extra food. Every family in the building had a small plot of land which most used to grow vegetables. At the suggestion of the landlady, I got work by digging some of these little garden plots for people in our own building and eventually other buildings too. While some people paid me in cash, I would have preferred payment in food. On one occasion, one woman had just finished cooking some chicken noodle soup and asked if I would like to have some as payment. I had a plate and was offered another. The soup was excellent. It had been freshly made and was of normal peacetime standard with pieces of chicken, noodles and vegetables. Eventually, I had three full plates. She was astonished that I had eaten so much but also then generously gave me a half a loaf of bread and half a dozen sticks of rhubarb for only two hours' work. This was quite a contrast to some of the other payments I had received.

Apart from work, there wasn't much in Bielefeld to do. Although you could go swimming during the summer, there were generally only two types of entertainment, one of which was going to the sideshow fair on the main town square which had rides and shooting galleries for prizes. But it was expensive for us teenage boys who had little money. The other alternative was going to the cinema which, at one Reichsmark per movie, was affordable. The movies were categorised by age group and sometimes my friends and I would sneak into the movies intended for older age groups or adults. We got caught a few times, but when the police asked for our names so they could write up their report we gave them made-up and outrageous-sounding Polish names like Caczmakovski or Kulidupski. Being western Germans, they were not used to hearing names like this so they had no idea that we were deceiving them. You could also see on the policemen's faces that they had no idea how to spell the name, so they ended up just giving us a warning and sending us on our way.

Winter 1946–47

The winter of 1946–47 was one of the coldest on record. The summer of 1946 had been hot and dry, and drought conditions had affected what few crops had been possible and this led to a bad harvest. Then suddenly in November the temperature sank to under freezing throughout Europe and so began the worst winter in quite some time. Temperatures fell to minus 30 degrees Celsius and this lasted all the way through until March 1947.

By January, the Rhine River froze for 60 kilometres in the French and British occupation zones. The River Elbe froze completely, which meant no supplies could be delivered by ship, while much of the remainder of the transportation system had, of course, been destroyed by bombing. There was also some talk of the English Channel being frozen up to one kilometre away from the coastline.

The situation was most serious in the Western occupation zones, where 60 per cent of the German population lived. Before the war, these zones had been the most heavily industrialised area of Germany and only about 40 per cent of the country's food had been produced there. Furthermore, as one of the most heavily bombed areas, war damage and the loss of farm workers also had a dramatic effect on food production in these zones. Known as the time of *weisser Tod* (the white death), and *schwarzer Hunger* (the black hunger), the situation was particularly critical in the cities, and many hundreds of thousands died from cold, hunger and illness; the young and old were particularly vulnerable.

Anything and everything was bartered. No animal was safe and harvested fields would be searched again and again for any left-over vegetables. Valuable property, jewellery and whatever was of value was exchanged for food. Many farmers took unfair advantage of this, as did some occupation troops, while black marketeers and speculators took whatever they could of what was available, but for ordinary people the most important thing was survival.[15]

Everything capable of being used as fuel was taken, and people would

Me as a 16-year-old, winter 1946–47. (Otto Gaczol)

walk for hours to find trees which still had branches. On top of that, there were no proper coal deliveries that winter. What we did receive was damp coal dust which had the texture of clay and was unusable in that form. To get it to burn, you had to have an already existing fire to dry out the coal dust before you could use it. So people started to steal coal from the rail yards. A soon as a train carrying coal came in, people would descend upon it, grab whatever coal they could and make a run for it as soon as possible before the police arrived. The local German police were easy to spot as their cars and vans travelled at the usual speed and, due to a shortage of globes, had only one light shining – on the left-hand side – so you were unlikely to get caught. It also seemed to me that the police didn't make any sort of special effort to catch us either. Perhaps they accepted the reality of the situation that the people stealing the coal weren't organised criminals, rather they were just desperate and cold.

Even lawyers and, indeed, one judge got caught stealing coal. The British occupation MPs, on the other hand, were very serious about stopping the theft and their vehicles sped to the railway yards to apprehend people. If you got caught, you went to court but there was no criminal record.

The theft of goods became so bad that eventually it received official, though conditional, forgiveness by the Church. At the end of December 1946, the then Archbishop (later Cardinal) Josef Frings[16] of Cologne gave his blessing to those who had to steal in order to feed or warm their families. Archbishop Frings did, however, add that whatever was taken had to be replaced or reimbursed as soon as possible. Nonetheless, his endorsement added a new word to the vocabulary of the local Kölsch dialect: *fringsen* – stealing for a legitimate reason.[17]

In April 1947, spring finally arrived and although the bitter cold ended, the hunger did not. The situation improved but the summer of 1947 was also very hot and the harvest failed again. Food shortages continued until the summer of 1948.[18]

Starting work

My mother found me an apprenticeship with her company, Anker-Werke AG, at the second of their two plants (Werke II) in Bielefeld in June 1946. She already had a good relationship with the general manager in Bielsko-Biala and it was through him that I was given the position of milling machinist. Although I had wanted to be a car mechanic, positions like that weren't available unless you were very well connected. Indeed, all apprenticeships were rare and I was lucky to get the job particularly as I had no idea of what it was and even less idea about anything to do with engineering.

The apprenticeship was for two years only with payment of 25 Reichsmarks per month for the first year, and 35 Reichsmarks per month for the second. Apart from the pay itself, the company did try to provide other support to its employees as the money itself couldn't buy much. It appears that the company were also on the black market and they shared with us the goods they procured. For example, one day we all got three lemons and on another we got preserved herrings – two for married men and one for singles.

I worked hard during my time as an apprentice and tried to show initiative by learning as much as I could. Frustrated by what seemed to me to be boring production work, I eventually asked my supervising tradesman and foreman to give me more challenging work, such as setting up the machines for milling rather than just watching the milling work itself. I had already keenly watched all the operations that I could, so it wasn't hard for me to pick up the extra tasks. In the end, I was promoted to working in the tool room and I was very proud to have been chosen to do so. There, my new supervising tradesman paid me extra attention and I successfully completed my apprenticeship within the two years. Of the four of us who started our apprenticeship together, one left to work for his father's transport company, while the other two didn't complete their certificates.

Mother's new man

My mother had, in the meantime, met a guy who she was very enthusiastic about. He had been in a POW camp in the UK, but ended up in Bielefeld. I didn't like him at all and his immediate invitation to address each other by first name and use the 'du'[19] of intimacy was not something I welcomed or agreed to. In the end I was right: he couldn't be trusted and eventually used my mother. For example, when the new Deutschmark (DM) currency was introduced, everyone was given 40 DM and a few weeks later another 20 DM. My mother asked me to give her the 40 DM for her new man to get some dental work done. Much to my regret, I gave her the money – money I could have used to buy some much-needed shoes or shirts. Eventually his unsavoury history came out. He had been working for the German army as a supply officer and he had been selling army equipment, such as boots, clothing and food, on the black market and had been caught. Specifically, he had been apprehended for trying to sell a truck's worth of potatoes. He had escaped custody but in the meantime had been sentenced to death in absentia. Eventually he made his way to Italy through Czechoslovakia, where he had surrendered himself to the British armed forces. He told them he was Polish and took a Polish name. He was then sent to a POW camp in the UK and was released after the war. He then returned to Germany where he met my mother.

After the establishment of German political parties, he went from one to another lobby to have his death sentenced quashed but they all rejected him – even the German Communist Party knocked him back. He eventually found a job as a night-watchman somewhere. My mother was besotted with him and spoiled him, even to the point of buying only white bread for him, which was quite a luxury at the time. Their general relationship and her desire to marry him created tension between us. After an argument with him, I got kicked out of the house but after three months my mother turned up at the farm where I was working and invited me back home. She had kicked him out after he had met another woman and ended their relationship.

The 'cigarette and chocolate-bar' economy and the Deutschmark

With no functioning government and a shortage of goods and foodstuffs, the post-war German economy largely reverted to barter on the black market. About half the goods in Germany were swapped on this black market and the currency that had been in circulation under the Nazi regime – the Reichsmark – was eliminated from these transactions and replaced by goods; most notably cigarettes and chocolate bars, but also alcohol.[20]

It was terrible living during the three years of the 'cigarette and chocolate-bar' economy. All consumer goods were either difficult or impossible to come by. In the two years I was with my mother in Bielefeld, I never had one of my requisitions for clothes or shoes filled. When stories went around about consumer items that were about to be put on sale, people would start lining up overnight so that they would be at the head of the line when the offices or shops opened at 8 a.m. the following day. Even then, there was no guarantee you would get what you had waited for.

Picking up cigarettes was big business as US soldiers only smoked half, and children and teenagers like me would follow them around waiting for them to discard their half-smoked butts. We would then pick them up and sell them on. During my Nuremberg visit in February 1946, I waited around the opera house, where the Americans would gather, and managed to collect quite a number of unsmoked and half-smoked cigarettes. That haul, plus my own unsmoked German cigarettes, netted me a total of 150 Reichsmarks. While this wasn't much, it was still a good result as cash remained necessary for some transactions.

Opera House, Nuremberg, where in February 1946 I used to wait to pick up cigarettes discarded by US soldiers. Photo taken in 2005. (Andrew Gaczol)

When currency reform finally occurred and the Deutschmark was introduced in June 1948, it was a welcome change. By chance, this was also at about the time I finished my apprenticeship. There had been many rumours flying around about currency reform for quite some time and people had become very sceptical. However, this time it was true.

Businesses at that time were not prepared to make their goods available while the currency question was unresolved. They were simply not prepared to swap their valuable goods for a currency – the Reichsmark – that was now essentially useless paper. So when the new, credible Deutschmark appeared on Sunday, 20 June 1948, the shops literally overnight became full of consumer goods which had hitherto been unavailable or in very short supply. Tarpaulins had been placed over the shop windows but on Monday 21 June, they were pulled away to reveal an array of goods: shoes, bikes, sewing machines – all were there. Cars and white goods, though, were still in short supply and food was still rationed. We had to wait until January 1950 to see the end of food rationing.

The DM's introduction effectively crystallised the Cold War between the west and the Soviet Union. The western Allies and the USSR were already bickering well before June 1948 and by the end of 1947 almost all forms of cooperation had already broken down. During 1947, the US and British zones were economically and administratively amalgamated into a Bizone or Bizonia in order to foster economic recovery. The Bizonia operated through a set of German institutions located in Frankfurt am Main and its federative structure would later serve as the model for West Germany.[21] In June 1947, the Soviets established the German Economic Commission with the idea of centralising the Soviet-zone economy. The London Conference of Foreign Ministers during November-December 1947 failed, as the four countries could not agree on a common policy and by 20 March 1948, the Soviets had walked out of the Allied Control Council (ACC).[22] So when the DM was introduced into the western sectors, effectively dividing Germany economically, the USSR responded on 24 June 1948 by blocking all road and rail traffic into West Berlin. This was the start of the Berlin Blockade and ultimately the Berlin Airlift. By May 1949, the western Allies had agreed to allow the formation of the Federal Republic of (West) Germany – the Bundesrepublik – and the new state was proclaimed on 23 May 1949. In August 1949, the USSR exploded its first atomic bomb and, in response to the Bundesrepublik's foundation, the Soviet Union gave its blessing to the establishment of the (East) German Democratic Republic – the DDR – on 7 October 1949. The Cold War was definitely on.

German rearmament – *Ohne Uns*

The entrenchment of the Cold War saw a desire by the western powers to rearm the new Bundesrepublik. Even as early as 1950, the United States was pressuring France to accept a rearmed West Germany on its border. The member states of the North Atlantic Treaty Organisation (NATO) were also in favour of rearmament, except the French and Belgian governments. The majority of public opinion, too, especially in France, did not seem ready to accept a new German army, as memories of World War II and of German occupation were still fresh in their memory.[23] But German public opinion was also against it. Both world wars had resulted in Germany's defeat and, in the case of the second, the utter devastation of the majority of Germany's cities and a complete foreign occupation. There was very little appetite in West Germany for

My Personalausweis (identity card), which was issued to me when the Federal Republic of Germany was established in May 1949. (Andrew Gaczol)

rearmament or another war and the *Ohne Uns* (without us or count us out) anti-war movement developed.[24]

My recollection was that the initial proposal was that a German corps or a German legion with German soldiers under the command of US officers be formed. But this was rejected. Eventually the Sozialdemokratische Partei Deutschlands (Social Democratic Party of Germany) or SPD dropped its opposition to rearmament and supported the conservative government of Konrad Adenauer in the formation of a new defence force on 12 November 1955. The name was officially designated Bundeswehr (Federal Defence Force) on 1 April 1956 and three months later conscription was introduced.[25] Although my passport application and eventual decision to leave West Germany occurred at the same time the decision was made to form the Bundeswehr, the two events were coincidental. Although at 23 years old I was already too old to be conscripted, I would have done my national service had I been called upon to do so. Indeed, I may very well have volunteered as I still had the idea at that time that I would have liked to have been in the Luftwaffe.

Working for Dr Hünerhof

My landlady, who had previously helped me get gardening work with our neighbours, also helped me get some extra work with a doctor by the name of Hünerhof who owned a two-acre farm. Dr Hünerhof's father had been indirectly killed by the Nazis. The Gestapo had arrested him after he made a comment against the regime and, as a result, they had placed him in a bomb disposal unit where he had eventually been killed when one of the dud aerial bombs dropped by the Allies exploded. I went to meet Dr Hünerhof and his family, and we sat down and discussed the work arrangements. There was plenty of work to be done and we agreed that I would be paid 50 Pfennigs per hour and that I would also be fed. But the meal was to cost 50 Pfennigs. So, I would work for three hours or so, get payment of one Reichsmark and 50 Pfennigs, but would go home with one Reichsmark in my pocket and a full stomach. There I learnt to cut grass with a scythe and dig their vegetable plots. Eventually he suggested that I resign from my apprenticeship and take up a job with him full-time. Given that I was lucky to have the apprenticeship and I felt that it was important to get a trade behind me, I said no but told him I would reconsider working for him when my apprenticeship ended.

In May 1948, I finished my apprenticeship and I went back to Dr Hünerhof to take up his offer of employment. The contract with Dr Hünerhof had to be signed by him, myself and my mother as at that time 21 was the age that one became a legal adult in Germany. They paid me 20 DM a month for the first year, and 35 DM per month during the second year. The pay wasn't much, but I was also treated as part of the family in what in Germany is called *Familieinanschluss*. This meant that I got food and accommodation as well having my washing done.

Dr Hünerhof had inherited the house and wanted to renovate it. It was two storeys high, quite old, and with an old-fashioned drop toilet. There was no plumbing, which meant no sewerage and no proper bathroom. As the Hünerhof family were considered Nazi victims due to their father being indirectly killed by the regime, they received preferential treatment in terms of education and access to goods and materials. So Dr Hünerhof used this access to get cement and other materials to fully renovate the building. I learnt quite a lot there. I learnt to lay bricks, and lay water pipes and gas pipes, all the while working with Fritz, Dr Hünerhof's brother. We installed a bathroom with a shower and wash basin and I also learnt to lay ceramic tiles. The really tough job was connecting the sewerage. The existing mains were five metres deep and I was the one who ended up digging the ditch from the house to the street to complete the connection. It was actually rather dangerous, as there were no wooden bracings or supports to stop the side walls collapsing on top of you. Good health, occupation and safety practices weren't a major consideration in post-war Germany.

I worked for Dr Hünerhof for two years until April 1950, when I eventually got bored with the work. The wages never increased and 35 DM per month was very little. For example 35 DM was enough to buy only a pair of shoes and nothing else. A suit cost 100 DM and it eventually took me four months to save the money until I could buy one. It got to the point where the Hünerhof family were sick of me hanging around because I didn't want to go out anywhere, as the money spent to do so would have meant that I would have to wait another month before I could buy the suit. In the end I asked for a raise to 60 DM per month, but that was something they couldn't afford. I sometimes wonder if they were wasted years as I could, perhaps, have been doing something

Me at Anker-Werge AG, 1952. (Otto Gaczol)

more interesting or profitable. But what I learnt there stood me in good stead many years later when I owned my own home in Australia. Many of the repairs and renovations I did there were possible because of the experience I had gained working for the Hünerhofs.

Despite leaving their employ, I stayed on good terms with the Hünerhofs throughout my remaining time in West Germany. Even after I started my new job, I would still help out by picking fruit for them when they were desperate for labour and I was invited to celebrate Christmas with them every year. Dr Hünerhof eventually went on to become an X-ray specialist. As we were both born in the same month, the doctor – 10 years older than me – and I to this day still swap birthday phone calls every year.

Return to work at Anker-Werke AG

As it turned out, Anker-Werke AG was again looking for workers, and a milling machinist tradesman place was available. I applied for the job and I was very happy when I got it. Although my contract with Dr Hünerhof required that I give six weeks' notice, Anker-Werke AG generously held the job for me until those six weeks were over. While there was some talk that I might be able to leave the Hünerhof's after only two weeks, they eventually did ask me to work the full six. I was under the impression that Fritz had exerted a bit of pressure on his family for me to fulfil the full obligation. So, I started back at Anker-Werke AG after Easter 1950 – which fell on 9 April that year – with a wage of 48 DM per week.

In 1951, I joined the SPD, the centre-left party that represented workers (its Australian equivalent is the Australian Labor Party).[26] I must admit I joined mainly for pragmatic reasons – for example, being a member made it easier to find accommodation – but I took my membership seriously and regularly attended meetings and conferences even though I had no political ambitions as such. Although I had little sympathy for the communists, I felt that supporting the labour movement and workers' rights was important and I remained an SPD member right up until my departure for Australia in 1955.

Having found a new job, I settled into the usual work routine at Anker-Werke AG. But being still young, I wanted to see the world and I began to think about travelling. There had to be more to life than just Bielefeld.

Five

Decision to Travel

Boyhood dreams...

It was always my intention to travel. Even at 10 years of age, I had wanted to travel, as I had read many books about foreign countries and, although they were old books, I was fascinated. Initially, I had wanted to go to Africa as there had been an intention by the Nazi regime to reclaim the lost German colonies after what was expected to be a successful war. Nazi Germany even had an organisation which was looking for young people to train for life in Africa – the *Reichskolonialbund* (Reich Colonial League) or RKB. I joined, but it was eventually wound up in 1943 as the war was being lost and the RKB had become irrelevant.[1] Similarly, Hitler's aims for *Lebensraum* (living space) in eastern Europe and the Soviet Union – the Generalplan Ost – was supposed to result in German colonies and colony cities in these conquered territories.[2] As a boy during the war, I had intended to relocate myself there as a farmer to this 'Greater Germany'. So the idea of travelling and seeing the world was always part of my agenda.

...and post-war plans

Despite the dreams of travel and adventure, I had no intention of leaving Germany permanently, and Australia as a destination was initially not part of my plan at all. I just wanted to travel. At the time, there was no such thing as tourism as we know it today, so emigrating for a period was the way a young person could see the world. Fortunately, a number of countries had liberalised their immigration policies in the immediate post-war period, partly to accommodate the refugees created by the conflict and partly to provide a stimulus to their own economies, and this gave me the opportunity to pursue my travel ambitions. At first, I wanted to go to South Africa but ,given the racial/political situation there, I felt that this was not a viable option. Although segregation had existed long before, the Apartheid state had just been established in 1948[3] and I expected that eventually the black African population would revolt against the minority whites. This sort of political unrest was not something I wanted to experience, so I then looked towards North America.

Already in the second half of 1948, there had been an advert in the newspapers looking for young men to crew the Liberty ships[4] from the United States to Europe. The idea of being a sailor didn't bother me and I was very enthusiastic to be able to leave Germany, see the world and have an adventure. As instructed by the advert, I went to the *Arbeitsamt* (employment office) as quickly as I could. The official there, however, tried to talk me out of it and even denied having seen the advert. Eventually he became terse, almost accusing me of being some form of traitor for wanting to work for the Allies. I couldn't have cared less: as far as I was concerned, the war was over and I just wanted to get on with my life. In the end, I got no information from him and left the *Arbeitsamt* with nothing to show for my efforts.

In 1950, there was again an advert in the newspapers. This time, it was for an immigration program to the United States. Already in 1948, the Displaced Persons Act of 1948 allowed for 'admission into the United States of certain European displaced persons for permanent residence'[5] so there was a possibility that I would be able to settle there. Once again, I was very enthusiastic and presented myself to the *Arbeitsamt*. This time, they confirmed the programme and gave me the necessary paperwork so that I could apply. But that was also the time of the Korean War.

In June 1950, the armed forces of North Korea invaded South Korea and the United Nations, led by the United States, intervened on behalf of the South. Having heard a rumour that the United States drafted foreign nationals living in the US into their armed forces, I did not want to find myself drafted as a soldier and fighting for the US on the Korean peninsula. Although the US occupation forces in Germany were generally well behaved, they did have a habit of calling us young boys 'little Nazis' and this still rankled with me. As it turns out, the rumours were true – you could be drafted as a foreign national to serve in the US military.[6]

By 1952, my mother had developed a lung illness and eventually spent a total of five years in a sanatorium or health clinic, so I never returned to her home to live when I finished working for Dr Hünerhof. Although living quarters were hard to find, I luckily found an unfurnished room just five minutes' walk from the Anker-Werke AG factory. I took the bed from my mother's home, as she was still at the health clinic. Over a period for four years, I slowly bought myself other furniture, such as a nice sofa bed, as well as a small table and chairs ensemble and a wireless set. It was a little unusual, as a young man in his early 20s, for me to be living alone, as many West German men my age got married at 21 in order to get away from their parents. At that time, I had no interest in getting married as I was employed, had money in my pocket and wanted to enjoy myself after having just lived through the war's end and the difficult years immediately thereafter.

The rent was cheap and I stayed there for four years, only having to move out a few months before my eventual departure to Australia. These few months saw me move into more expensive but still convenient lodgings.

Almost Canada

At about that time, I met a guy at Anker-Werke AG called Ewald who had hailed from the old East Prussian city of Königsberg (today Kaliningrad in the Russian Federation). He had lost his parents in a bombing raid and we began to talk and occasionally go out together. A bit of a rogue, he dressed badly and on our first night out was rather rude to the girls, expecting them to buy him beer. Although I wasn't convinced everything he told me was true, he said that he had a brother in the United States who worked as a pilot for an American airline. Eventually Ewald told me that he was applying to emigrate to Canada as his brother had advised him that getting to the United States was easy once you had been accepted into Canada.[7] So he applied and, in March 1954, he left West Germany for Canada. I, too, applied for Canada but by the time I received my immigration number, that year's intake was complete. Offers to travel were restricted from March to October as there was no work available during winter. The Canadian authorities, though, told me that I would be included in the next call-up for immigrants.

'Populate or perish' – Australia calling

Alone again and waiting to hear from the Canadians, another workmate told me of his application to go to Australia. At the time, I had no idea that Australia was a potential destination for immigrants. After World War II the Australian government committed itself to a vigorous and sustained immigration program. During the war, the threat of Japanese attack had made the country realise that the continent was largely unpopulated and that in order to better defend itself, a bigger population was needed. From this, the slogan 'populate or perish' was born.[8] Apart from defence, the immigration program was also designed to meet labour shortages and stimulate the economy. As a result, from 1945 to 1975, about three million migrants and refugees arrived in Australia and the population almost doubled from seven and a half million to 13 million.[9] On 29 August 1952, the Australian government signed an emigration agreement with the West German government. This agreement allowed 10,000 Germans to emigrate to Australia in 1953. The quota of 10,000 was to consist of 4,000 workers (3,000 from agriculture and 1,000 skilled industrial workers) and 6,000 family members of those workers.[10] Despite being enemies during the war, the Australian government was generally enthusiastic for Germans to come to Australia and it was, in a sense, competing with Canada for access to a large pool of skilled labour. Immigration minister in the then Menzies government, Harold Holt, said during his visit to Europe in 1952, 'Some excellent potential migrants are to be found in Germany, including very many skilled tradesmen and other specialists in the categories we need... there is an unusually qualified reservoir of human material here.'[11] Given that I had just become a tradesman, I certainly fitted the bill.

Having heard of my workmate's application, I once again returned to the *Arbeitsamt* to apply for Australia's immigration scheme. To be eligible to get the government-assisted passage, one had to commit to staying for at least two years. So my intention was to go to Australia, save money and then eventually travel to the United States. As a point of interest, although I would also have considered New Zealand as an option, it wasn't readily accepting German immigrants at that time as it was focused on appealing to British immigrants and, to a lesser extent, the Dutch.[12]

When I finished filling out the papers, the *Arbeitsamt* asked if I was married and explained that the Australian immigration authorities preferred married men with families to those who were still single. Leaving my chances to fate, I told him to lodge the application anyway.

Just after I lodged my application for Australia I suddenly started receiving letters from Ewald in Canada. This surprised me a little, as we had fallen out a bit before he left: his rudeness and slothful ways had gotten the better of me. He apologised for his behaviour and invited me to come over to Canada and join him. He had only been there for six months but was doing well and had already bought himself a car. He offered to pay my fare – which was about 800 DM – on the condition that I pay him back after my arrival. I would have been quite happy to do that, but in the meantime I had been invited by the Australian authorities for a medical check-up. The process with the Australian authorities was then finalised and, by the time I started dating my future wife, I already knew that my trip to Australia was a real possibility. On top of that, contact with Ewald had once again gone cold and I had already started to write off the Canada option. Fate again played its hand: just one week after I left for Australia, a letter from Ewald arrived in Bielefeld telling me that all the arrangements from his side were finalised and that I could now make my way over to Canada. Had this letter arrived earlier, I would have gone. It was, however, too late as I was already on my way to Australia.

Romance and engagement

Having made the decision to travel, I knew that I'd need as much money as I could scrape together before I left. So I stayed home and saved what I could. Although I still went to the movies, I spent nothing on anything extravagant.

But six weeks of sitting home can take its toll, especially when you are 23 years old. Boredom ensued, and I decided that it was time to step out and go dancing, if only occasionally. Bielefeld's main industries manufactured sewing machines and business machines, as well as textiles such as shirts. These industries hosted dances and one evening I went to a dance hall and there was a young girl who worked as a seamstress with one of her girlfriends (who coincidentally also eventually emigrated to

Canada) and another guy. I had known this girl by sight for a long time. I had first seen her during the hot summer of 1947, as lots of people used to attend the local swimming pool. As a swimming club member, she had swept me up in her wake as she swam laps and exited the pool from the stairs. Fate would have it that we would see each other around Bielefeld at least once a year and, as it turns out, we also had some mutual friends. So by the time I met her at the dance in September 1954 we already 'knew' each other.

I asked her to dance and she said yes. Custom had it that when one finished the dance one would then ask, 'Can I have the next dance?' and if there was interest the young lady would say yes. Although shy, she kept saying yes, and we kept dancing together all night and we then finished the evening with a liqueur nightcap. I then asked if I could walk her home, and we did. From that point, we were a couple.

When I eventually got the final confirmation for my trip to Australia, I took my new girlfriend out on a Saturday and broke the news about my impending travel. I explained that this was not necessarily the end of our relationship. I made it clear that she was more than welcome to come with me to Australia, but that it was her choice. Although she didn't show it, she was not very happy. But she suggested I speak with her parents about our options and I was invited to their home to do so. So, with my 11 DM bunch of flowers for her mother and a 1 DM cigar for her father (which was a fair bit of money for me, given I was only earning 60 DM per week at the time) I arrived on the following Sunday to meet her parents and get their reaction to the idea of taking their daughter to the other side of the world. Her father put me through a friendly but thorough interrogation about what sort of person I was, rather than the specific idea of his daughter coming with me to Australia. Her mother kept trying to get us back on track about Australia but he persisted and responded by saying we could talk further about that during future visits.

In the end, I left it for my girlfriend to decide but I felt that if she were to follow me, we should get engaged. Although we could have gotten married and I could have delayed my departure, it would have been awkward in terms of my existing application. The other option was that, as the commitment to Australia was for two years, I could have returned to West Germany should I not have liked it there and we could have been married upon my return. My girlfriend decided to follow me and we were engaged on Christmas Day 1954.

My future parents-in-law were happy with our engagement but there was at least once voice of minor dissent in the family. With family names like Neumann and Hoffman in the family tree, my fiancée's heritage was entirely German. Upon hearing of his niece's engagement, one of the family's uncles questioned my background given the Polish family name of Gaczol. Although reassured by my future mother-in-law, he wasn't entirely happy.

Although I did eventually invite my mother to the engagement party, it was essentially at the request of my future mother-in-law. Our relationship had become somewhat distant and although I visited her from time to time and we talked, we were at that point leading separate lives.

Auf Wiedersehen from West Germany

After celebrating our engagement at Christmas, I spent the final two weeks in West Germany at my future parents-in-laws' house sleeping on the settee in the kitchen. This was a generous offer by them as it saved me a number of weeks' rent. All this caused a flurry of gossip as I was spied by the other tenants of the building going to the bathroom located on the landing just off the staircase.

My fiancée and I celebrated *Silvester* (New Year's Eve) at my future brother-in-law's apartment and, on 16 January 1955, she accompanied me to the main railway station in Bielefeld, where I began my long trip to Australia. My first destination was the emigration camp in Munich, where I spent four days. Although some of us looked around the city itself, it was still midwinter and cold, so we didn't see much. From there, we went by train to Genoa in Italy. Normally, departure from West Germany would have been from Bremerhaven but my ship, the MS *Seven Seas*, needed to have its engine repaired at Marseilles, so its departure was rescheduled and relocated to Genoa. The train trip between Munich and Genoa was incredible. The sights we saw out of the windows looked as though they had been taken from a picture postcard collection. The Alps were stunning, with small villages and their church spires dotted throughout the valleys adding to the extraordinary vistas. One sunset in particular was unforgettable as all the mountain tops were covered in a pink glow from the slowly fading sunlight.

At the Brenner Pass, we stopped and bought some wine from a local Italian villager. As it was winter, he must have been freezing standing out there with his cart but he sold a few bottles to a number of people on the train and he must have made quite a few lira that night. The wine itself was also freezing but it eventually warmed up and a spontaneous Italian wine-fuelled party broke out with lots of singing and laughing. One guy had brought a trumpet with him, and the wine and stunning scenery inspired him to blast out a few tunes.

Sailing the Seven Seas

In the morning, we arrived at the port and went straight from the train to the MS *Seven Seas*. At the time it was a Norwegian ship, Panama-flagged but with a German crew, and had a colourful history as a cargo ship, troop ship and an auxiliary aircraft carrier during World War II. Built in the United States during 1940–41, it was about 13,500 tons, 150 metres in length and could make 17 knots. It could carry about a thousand passengers, almost all of whom on my voyage were immigrants.[13] As both we and the ship got ready to depart, the ship's engines caused the ship to vibrate and much to my astonishment I began to feel seasick. I couldn't believe it. Despite my instinct to the contrary, one of the other guys advised me to eat something to settle my stomach and I went to the

MS *Seven Seas*, my ship to Australia. *(Canadian Museum of Immigration DI2013.534.1)*

Me on deck, about to depart Genoa, January 1955.
I'm looking a little unsteady because of seasickness. (Otto Gaczol)

ship's dining room to see if I could get a meal. As it was quite common, the galley staff weren't bothered at all by my request and provided me with some food which did the trick. I was also quite lucky to get a cabin in the middle of the ship on A deck, which meant that I didn't have to suffer the worst of the ship's motion as it rose and fell through the ocean waves.

In my six-bunk share cabin was one of the few private passengers (as opposed to us immigrants), who looked down on us a little; there was also an elderly couple and, in the bunk immediately below me, was a chap called Gerhardt who hailed from Opele (Oppeln) in Upper Silesia, not far from my home town. Gerhardt and I established a friendship on board which then lasted for many years in Australia. In Genoa, about 200 to 300 Austrian and Germans came on board, as well as some Italians, and between us we occupied the ship's upper decks. Most of the Germans were single, and most were men – there were only about seven single German girls. By an unbelievable coincidence, one of those girls was a niece of the farmer I worked for in Bavaria immediately after the war. When I told her that I thought her uncle was a bit of a bastard, she readily agreed. It really is a small world.

From Genoa we went down to the port of Athens, Piraeus. There, you won't be surprised to learn that many Greeks came on board and it seemed to me that many were farmers and villagers from some of the poorer parts of Greece. While in port, it was possible for passengers to go ashore and visit the Acropolis. Uncertain, I dithered and by the time I had decided to go it was too late, as all passengers had to be back on board one hour before departure. From the ship, we could see that a movie was being filmed in the port area. My recollection was that it was the British film *Doctor in the House*, but that film was released before January 1955. Nonetheless, there was something being filmed there and it was quite interesting to see it all happen. This included the particularly beautiful young Greek women who played the extras.

We were only in Piraeus for a day or so, if I remember correctly. In the evening, we left to sail toward the Suez Canal. The canal trip itself was uneventful and we arrived at Port Suez, where the ship stopped to complete various bureaucratic requirements. While the ship was waiting, the local Egyptians would come up to the ship in their rowing boats and try to sell shoes and other leather goods. The Egyptians would throw a rope up to the ship and pass up a shoe for inspection to the prospective buyer. But they would only send one, with the second coming only after payment had been provided. Sadly, some of passengers didn't send down the payment after the second shoe arrived and the Egyptians got ripped off. Eventually an Egyptian policeman – who, with a rifle and ammunition pouches, looked more like a soldier – came on board to try to stop it.

After we left Port Suez, we arrived at Aden in Yemen. There, we met many enthusiastic taxi drivers who were lined up at the port and very willing to drive us the 15 kilometres or so to the city itself – for a price, of course. One offered to take five of us to the city for one pound sterling and we agreed. But we had misunderstood, as we had thought he had meant Australian pounds. When our journey with him was finally over, we couldn't pay the full fee, as Australian pounds were worth about two shillings less than a British pound. Although he complained and it was a bit embarrassing for us, we paid him the Australian pound upon our return to the ship. Incidentally, I also had with me some Deutschmarks, and they were readily accepted as payment right up until Aden.

Aden itself was full of people and, although it seemed to us to be quite chaotic, it had a certain aromatic order to it. Pedestrians and vehicles shared the roads and despite the loud honking of horns, people got to where they needed to go and so did the vehicles. One of the German girls with us was from Hamburg and she was your archetypal blonde bombshell: tall, blonde and blue-eyed. The Arabs were entranced by her and kept pinching her bottom. Eventually us guys formed a protective ring around her so she would no longer be harassed. The aromas were quite incredible and we savoured 'all the smells of the Orient', as one would say back in Europe. We were also warned aboard ship to not drink liquids from open cups and that we should only buy canned or bottled drinks like Coca Cola so as to avoid getting sick. Even then we were warned that we should check that the seals on the cans and bottles were intact, as the local shopkeepers would often water down the product so as to get more sales out of their stock. Not wanting to take any risks, we didn't drink anything at all. We also had a small Arab man walk with us and eventually we realised that in his mind he was giving us a tour and he expected to be paid. Embarrassingly, we didn't pay him anything, as we had no small change and parting with an entire Australian pound was unthinkable as it was quite a lot of money in 1955.[14] One of the more curious things we saw was a petrol station which advertised itself as being open all day and all night. There were two bowsers, and between them was an improvised bed made of cotton straps and wooden legs. The business owner would sleep on that bed at night, rousing himself only when a customer pulled up and then going immediately back to sleep after they had left.

We left Aden and unfortunately had a couple of tragedies on board. A young Greek couple had brought a sick baby on board with them, even though they had been advised by the ship's doctor that this was very risky and that he would not be held responsible if anything went wrong. Sadly, the baby died. Even though they had been advised not to bring the child they, and the Greek passengers generally, were furious with the doctor for the child's death. Similarly, about one week later, a Greek man had his appendix removed and was advised by the doctor not to eat or drink for 24 hours. Again, the advice wasn't taken and he too died. Both were buried at sea and their deaths, amongst a few other squabbles, caused some tension between the Greek and German/Austrian passengers.

Despite this, we were generally looked after well by the ship's crew and while the food was nothing special it was certainly adequate. There were

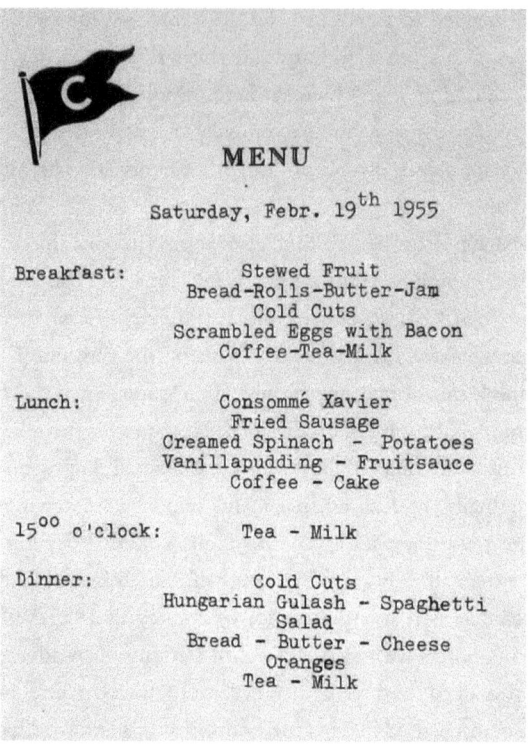

Menu card for our last night on board, 19 February 1955. (Otto Gaczol)

plenty of sandwiches, and coffee to drink, and everyone got a piece of fruit every day, which was normally an orange or apple. The frozen eggs, though, were a bit of a disaster and one evening we were served a mutton stew that was left entirely untouched: nobody ate it at all. We were also fed an endless stream of cauliflower, so much so that I didn't eat it again for years. Beer glasses were only half-full, but we got charged full price and until we arrived in Fremantle there were no soft drinks other than ginger beer. I also particularly remember the Austrians complaining to the Austrian consul upon their arrival in Melbourne that they hadn't been served dumplings on the month-long trip. This was serious business as dumplings are very popular in Austria. Never stand between an Austrian and their *Knödel*.

Apart from the unfortunate deaths, the only other drama during the trip was when we passed by the edge of a cyclone.[15] The ocean was very rough and for half a day the ship was buffeted by strong winds and big seas. As the ship ploughed its way through the ocean, its bow would rise high into the air and then come crashing down into the waves with the sound of cannon. While a number of people on board became seasick, it seemed that the Greeks were particularly susceptible. Some were so sick that they were crawling around on all fours. I have no idea why, but perhaps because many were from poor villages and had little previous chance to travel, they were not used to being on large ships on the open ocean.

My own private drama occurred when I awoke in the middle of the night to the sound of loud, horrific screams which then slowly faded away. It sounded to me that it had come from outside and I was worried that someone had fallen overboard and had screamed for help. I didn't react and became increasingly anxious that someone might have needed assistance and I had offered none. So the following morning I spoke with the chaps in the next cabin – which was also a six-berth dormitory-style cabin – about what I had heard and one of them explained that he was the culprit. Although a German citizen, he had been in the French Foreign Legion[16] and had fought in Vietnam at the decisive battle of Dien Bien Phu that lasted from late 1953 to May 1954.[17] He had had a nightmare that a Vietnamese soldier was coming to kill him and had screamed out during the night. I was relieved and thankful to hear that, as I had feared that my not reacting to the scream might have resulted in someone drowning.

By the end of the voyage, a sense of impatience engulfed the ship. The final week was very frustrating as there was little to do and we all just wanted to arrive and get on with our new lives. Just in time, the Western Australian port of Fremantle appeared over the horizon.

Six

Arrival in Australia

We arrived in Fremantle on 14 February 1955, a little less than a month after our departure from Europe. Upon our arrival, we were allowed to disembark for a few hours and have a look around. My friend Gerhardt bought himself a rockmelon but, unfamiliar with the fruit, he didn't know how to slice it, until eventually one of our shipmates showed him how it was done. I saw in an illuminated shop window a household sewing machine produced at Anker-Werke AG – the very same model that was made back in Bielefeld. I have to say that I was very proud to see something I had helped create here on the other side of the world.

By 11 p.m. we had returned to the ship and begun our journey across the Great Australian Bight to Melbourne. The weather was very rough and the ship itself seemed to have changed its characteristics: rather than heaving up and down, it was rolling from side to side, and quite severely too. At one stage, I began to wonder whether it would capsize. Despite the weather, we eventually reached Melbourne during the night of 19–20 February 1955 after a four-day journey.

Not so marvellous Melbourne

Melbourne then, as it is today, was Australia's second largest city after Sydney. In 1955, it had a population of about 1.5 million[1] and in the following year it hosted the Olympic Games. Having arrived at night, we had to wait until morning before we could disembark. When I woke up, I looked outside the porthole and thought, 'Wow, we're here!' All the passengers then got themselves ready to depart the ship and begin their new lives. Despite the initial excitement, my first impression was,

Standing on the dock at Port Melbourne, February 1955. (Otto Gaczol)

I must admit, not a good one. Waiting to disembark, I had retrieved my binoculars to take a proper look at the city. I was stunned by what I saw. There was public housing and cars, all of which looked old, run down and of pre-war vintage. I thought, 'Holy cow! Where on earth have I landed?' But as the contract with the Australian immigration authorities was for two years, it wasn't the end of the world even if it looked like it. I could even leave before the two years were up, but it would mean that I would have to pay my own fare – 80 pounds sterling – back to West Germany. Just in case, I had brought some goods with me, such as a quality camera, a silver fountain pen, a new alarm clock, silver cufflinks and a silver cigarette holder, that I could sell if I needed to. Fortunately, it never became necessary.

Before leaving West Germany, I met a guy who was leaving for Australia and he suggested that we meet upon my arrival. In fact, my fiancée and I saw him off from Bielefeld when he left. He had wanted to go to Queensland in the belief that it was all sun, no winter and lots of palm trees. This sounded good to me: at that time, all Europeans dreamed of a holiday in the South Pacific, with white sandy beaches and gently swaying palm trees. From the ship, I could see him on the dock. We called out to each other and he threw me an apple, exclaiming, 'I got a job and there's good money to be made here!' We agreed to meet after I had disembarked but somehow it never happened. I was very disappointed to have missed him and to this day I have no idea what happened to him.

Bonegilla

After our departure from the ship and processing by immigration officials, we were put on a train and sent to the Bonegilla Migrant Reception and Training Centre. During the journey, I looked out the window and observed the countryside. All of my observations reinforced the impression that I had formed when I first arrived in Melbourne: that most things were old, worn-out and of pre-war vintage. The cars were old, small and mostly English, which was a surprise as I had expected that Australia was more like the United States with large American cars on the road.

Bonegilla had become the main Australian migrant reception and training centre in 1947, and housed migrants until 1971. It was the largest and longest operating reception centre during the post-war era. The original camp covered 130 hectares and had very basic accommodation, with timber-framed, corrugated-iron army huts providing staff and migrants with housing, offices and communal kitchens, as well as dining and toilet facilities. New arrivals lived in Bonegilla while they were 'processed' and allocated jobs. It was also where non-English speakers could begin to learn English and Australian customs. Its intention was to help people make the transition to a new life in a new country.[2]

We arrived at the railway station in the late afternoon of Sunday 20 February and were asked by the Australian Federal Police to line up in rows, as one would be asked as a soldier in the army. Even though we could see the camp from the station and asked if we could just walk there – it would have taken about 20 minutes – we were told to wait until a bus arrived which would take us there. A couple of people started to walk but the officer politely but firmly called them back.

In 1952, riots had broken out because of the low level of camp amenities and poor conditions.[3] Before leaving West Germany, I had read an article written about a German woman who had returned from Australia describing the camp as very poor. But she had required treatment for cancer and that was also a factor in her homecoming. There were further riots in 1961, but this was more to do with the lack of work

Bonegilla, just before our departure on 25 February 1955. (Otto Gaczol)

than the conditions at the camp per se. The credit squeeze and recession of that year[4] meant that the migrants who had been promised work in Australia were left unemployed at Bonegilla for a long period and this was the main cause of the unrest.[5]

Upon our arrival, we were each given a basic bed with two blankets, and the doors were always left open – even after dark. At night we were also disturbed by possums scratching on the roof and didn't get much sleep. While it wasn't luxury accommodation, we all accepted it without complaint. We had wonderful breakfasts of bacon and eggs and received English lessons during the four full days I was there. We were all treated very well by all the officials who, by 1955, were well used to dealing with new arrivals from all over Europe. They were all very polite and didn't subject us to any prejudices because of our various nationalities, of which there were many.

One day, a group of us decided to go swimming in Lake Hume. As is the custom in Germany when men go swimming together, we went nude.

Indeed, in East Germany a nudist movement became established and was called the *Freikörperkultur* (Free Body Culture) or FKK. We thought nothing of it until one of the other migrants in the camp warned us that in Australia, swimming nude was not appropriate and that it might even result in us being arrested. This was an interesting introduction to some of the cultural differences between 1950s Australia and continental Europe.

In the end I spent only five days at Bonegilla. On the Thursday after we arrived, our English teacher asked us very politely if we were interested in volunteering to pick grapes as part of the upcoming harvest. Having been on a ship for four weeks, we were all quite restless and, having heard that some people had languished in Bonegilla for six months because of lack of work, we were all very keen to volunteer so that we could leave the camp as soon as possible.

Bound for South Australia

So early on Friday morning we were taken to the railway station and put on trains headed to Barmera in the first instance and then to Waikerie. We had at least one night on the train. For breakfast we had sandwiches, and the train stopped regularly for meals. All our food and transport was provided by the government as part of the immigration program.

One morning, we stopped at a station and there were many farmers milling about who asked us where we were going. There were about a dozen of us Germans, and when we responded that we were headed to Waikerie to pick fruit, they asked us to stay and pick fruit on their farms. At the time, we had no idea that we could accept their offer. With our well-developed German sense of *Ordnung*, we thought that as we were told we'd be going to Waikerie, then that's where we had to go. After all, we even had paperwork! The farmers, though, said, 'You're in Australia now. You can do what you want. You don't have to go to Waikerie. You can stay here with us if you like.' Despite this, we declined the offer. They wished us luck, but they were very disappointed, as they were quite keen for us to work for them.

Our train went through to Barmera and from there we were taken by bus to Waikerie. On our way, we had our first real Australian tucker: steak and egg with chips. We all thought it was wonderful. Waikerie itself is a

Doing the washing outside my accommodation, Waikerie. (Otto Gaczol)

small town in the Riverland area around the River Murray, where a large amount of Australia's fruit production occurs. Even today, Waikerie's population is only about 1,700 people;[6] in the mid-1950s, its population was probably only half of that.

The farmers then picked up the new immigrants from the employment station but I was one of the last to be picked, along with another guy from the MS *Seven Seas* whom I hadn't met on the ship. He was a barber from Hamburg and after chatting I discovered that he had done some travelling through Sweden. Our farmer then took us both to the pub. He spoke some German and was keen to improve it by speaking to us. This was a problem for me as I needed to improve my English and his enthusiasm for German wasn't going to help me get accustomed to my new home.

We were housed in a garage that had been converted into accommodation for use during the fruit harvest. It was comfortable enough with beds, a stove, and some basic furniture, and outside was a water tank for washing, all of which was completely adequate for our needs. My Hamburg friend also cut my hair when it needed to be done. As we arrived on Saturday, we both had the day off and, of course, Sunday as well. On Monday, we started work at 8 a.m.

After six weeks, some of the group I came with, including Gerhardt and my Hamburg friend, decided to leave Waikerie for Adelaide. I, however, wanted to stay in Waikerie until I had saved enough money for the fare back to West Germany should I feel the need to break the immigration contract before the mandatory two-year period. The wages were 11 Australian pounds 17 shillings per week, and after 12 weeks I had saved enough for the fare. Income tax was surprising low at only 17 shillings per week. I asked the farmer and he said, "Yes, it's low but if you're sick, or require a dentist or any other form of health care, you're on your own as there is no public health system in Australia.' If you were unlucky and got seriously sick, you would have to sell all your possessions to pay for your health bills. It wasn't until 1974–75 that the Whitlam government introduced a European-style universal health care system into Australia. In any case, all the migrants, as an incentive, had their taxes refunded after their first year. So in June I received my tax refund, which came to 40 Australian pounds, giving me a total of 120 Australian pounds in the bank.

Adelaide

After leaving Waikerie on my government-funded travel ticket, I looked for work in the South Australian capital, Adelaide. In 1955, Adelaide was a city of about half a million people, which is less than half its population today. In fact, the whole state of South Australia had less than 800,000 at the time.[7] Named after Adelaide of Saxe-Meiningen,[8] the German-born queen consort of the United Kingdom, Adelaide was founded in 1836. Apart from the name, there was also a strong history of German settlement in Adelaide and South Australia more generally.[9] Already in November 1838, the first settlers from Germany arrived because of religious persecution in their homeland. There are many German place names in South Australia – like Klemzig, Hahndorf and Lobethal – and South Australian wine-making has been strongly influenced by German traditions. Today, the Barossa Valley has a number of wineries with German names such as Langmeil, Peter Lehmann, Seppeltsfield and Wolf Blass.

But my arrival in Adelaide had nothing to do with this history. I was there simply to look for work after my time in Waikerie. Had I found similar fruit picking work in Victoria or elsewhere, I probably would have settled in Melbourne or one of the other state capitals instead. My other German friends, including Gerhardt, had found work at the railway repair yards at Islington, so it made sense to me to also go to Adelaide to look for work.

Adelaide's centre is laid out in a grid pattern which was then surrounded by parklands. These in turn were surrounded by the inner suburbs like Mile End to the west and Norwood to the east. As a new arrival, I was unfamiliar with the city centre so I set about orientating myself. Starting from the main train station on North Terrace, I would walk a city block: first to the left and then to the right so that I would always return to the main train station. As it was in a grid pattern, it didn't take me too long before I was able to find my way around.

Finding gainful employment...

Just after I first arrived, I went to the employment office and discussed my circumstances with an employment officer there who spoke some German. He gave me a list of places where I could apply for a job. On the top of the list was Perry Engineering[10] in Mile End, where there was a job vacancy for a second-class machinist with a wage of 14 Australian pounds 11 shillings. The start was almost immediate, but I needed to find some permanent accommodation and buy some working clothes.

As you can tell, at the time there was plenty of work available. Being bereft of the Queen's English wasn't a handicap either, as Australians had become quite used to non-English migrants looking for work. In many cases, communications were conducted through smiles, frowns and various forms of semaphore. This was during the post-war 'long boom'[11] and wherever you went there were big signs advertising for labour and many migrants had two jobs: the first which one would take seriously and a second job with which to earn extra money that one could be a bit slack at. It wouldn't matter if you lost it because you would find another second job soon enough.[12] In South Australia's case, there was also an activist state government under Premier Thomas Playford, who worked hard to establish industry and manufacturing.[13]

I spent two years at Perry Engineering doing a large variety of jobs, through which I vastly improved as a machinist. My supervisor, Bob, was a really fantastic boss. Although he had a gruff face, he was a thoughtful and considerate man with whom I got on well. One day, he was passing by just as I was finishing work. He asked where I was going, and I replied that I was heading to the tram stop on Henley Beach Road. He generously offered me a lift which I, of course, gratefully accepted. This is something that would never have happened in West Germany, where the division between management and workers was much more structured and formal.

...and suitable accommodation

The employment officer was very friendly and very helpful, helping me find not only employment, but also some comfortable and permanent accommodation. When I first arrived, he had already asked about my accommodation and I explained that Gerhardt was living in a hostel near the Islington railway station where he worked. I then got in touch with Gerhardt and asked for his help to find me an overnight stay but it was Adelaide Cup weekend – which fell on 14–16 May that year – and all the hotels were booked out. We went to the police station on Victoria Square that day and asked for some advice on where to find accommodation but the policeman on duty was rude and got very angry with us, asking us why we were bothering him. He felt that accommodation questions were out of his jurisdiction, and he informed us of his opinion very firmly. This was the only occasion that I was treated poorly by a government official. We then left and got some advice from a taxi driver at the taxi stand who then took me to a boarding house in Norwood where I stayed overnight.

I returned to the employment office the following day and the same officer went through the newspaper for me and found three potential accommodation options – all boarding houses. I then took another taxi to a different boarding house at 112 Edward Street, Norwood, which was run by an Australian couple. Thankfully they had a vacancy costing only five Australian pounds per week. This was a good price as it included my washing and all of my meals. Eventually I helped a guy called Kurt from the MS *Seven Seas* to also get some accommodation there. We shared a room and also spent lots of time together.

The boarding house could accommodate 10 boarders, but there were normally only six to eight. Of those staying there, most were Germans but

Elsie, Arthur and I heading for the beach, summer 1955–56. (Otto Gaczol)

there were also some Dutch and Indians. The couple who ran the boarding house – Elsie and Arthur – were originally from Albany in Western Australia, had a 20-year-old daughter and were on a working holiday to see Australia. At first I thought they were the owners of the building, but they only rented it. I'll explain more about that later. Elsie and Arthur were very decent and friendly people but I must admit I initially avoided Arthur as he was in the Australian army and had battled against Rommel's Afrika Korps in the North African campaign during World War II.[14] As he had fought against Nazi Germany, I tried to avoid him so as not to upset him in any way. One evening after a rain storm we ran into each other and he politely greeted me, and from then on our relationship grew. As part of the household chores, Arthur used to wash the dishes after the evening meal and, partly to get to know him better and partly out of a desire to improve my English, I offered to help him with the dish washing.

Eventually I got to know both Arthur and Elsie very well and they were incredibly friendly and helpful people. They would invite us to their friends' parties and they treated us as if we were their sons. Even as they themselves were leaving Adelaide, they gave us a lift to our own destination and it was quite an emotional send-off – Arthur looked like he had tears in his eyes. After their return to Albany, they also invited us to visit but being newly arrived migrants we really couldn't afford the plane tickets which, compared to today's prices, were quite expensive. The last time we heard from them was in 1957, about a year after my fiancée had arrived. Their cousin came to visit us and passed on their best wishes and an open invitation to visit. Sadly, we never did.

New country, new language

As a newly arrived migrant in Australia, I of course initially had a problem with language. It was incumbent upon us to learn English if we were to live in Australia successfully. To help us learn English, there was a government-funded language course that was, at the time, held behind the Old Parliament House on North Terrace. Later, it was moved to the new immigration offices on Kintore Avenue just off North Terrace near the State Library. The teacher had just returned from a European holiday that had included West Germany, and she was very positive about what she had seen there. If you did well at your lessons, she would say, 'You are my *Sonnenschein* (sunshine)!' She also explained that she enjoyed teaching the children of migrants as they picked up the lessons very quickly and in many cases faster than the local Australian children.[15]

At Perry Engineering, I had to work shifts, which left me at a disadvantage as I could not attend the lessons as often as I would have liked. My initial attempts to read the newspapers weren't successful but one of my friends had some English comic books. It may sound a bit strange, but those comic books really helped me, as I could match up the illustrated actions with the words in the captions. Within a few weeks, I reached a sufficient standard to be able to read a newspaper. However, I still needed to ask about certain words and phrases. I made a point of only asking my male friends, as I was never sure if one of the words I was asking about was in some way rude or embarrassing, particularly as Australians seemed to swear a lot.

Being a German in Australia

I didn't deliberately seek out other Germans to be friends with as there were plenty around. We naturally gravitated together and certainly

Gerhardt, my roommate Kurt and I spent a lot of time together. There were also a few others from MS *Seven Seas* as well. But I certainly didn't want to cut myself off and only have German friends. I felt that, coming to a new country, I should do my best to learn its ways and integrate myself as best as I could. Generally, I found Australians to be friendly and helpful despite the odd grumble of 'bloody migrants', and although I had heard that Australian girls wanted nothing to do with migrant men, I didn't find it to be entirely true. While they might have preferred Australian men, many went out with migrant men as well.

The only difficulty I had being a German was with a 20-year-old guy at Perry Engineering. Whenever he walked past those of us there who were Germans, he would give a Basil Fawlty-style Nazi salute and place two fingers under his nose in a mock Hitler moustache. When we asked why he did this, he replied, 'It's because of what you did to the Poles! The Polish people told me what you Germans did to them during the war!' I responded that while, yes, it was true, it was something he couldn't understand because he had not been there during those times. I also explained that those of us in Australia weren't responsible for those crimes as many of us, like myself, were only children at the time. He didn't care and continued to taunt and insult those of us who were German whenever he had the chance. Although I managed to ignore him for two weeks, in the end I lost my temper and was just about to belt him when my boss, Bob, came over and pulled me up. Actually, I expected to be fired but Bob was a gentleman and said, 'Don't be silly. This guy isn't worth it. He's a stupid kid. Ignore him.' Not long after that, the guy left, and I and the other Germans were left alone. The irony was that there were also Poles working at Perry Engineering with whom I got on quite well, especially when I told them that I had been born in Poland. The only exception was one Polish guy with whom I had had a misunderstanding over work arrangements, but that could have happened with anyone.

Shadows of the past

One day, Elsie took me aside and asked if I would like to meet the owners of the house in which we boarders were living. On an earlier occasion, she had explained to me, with an awkward look on her face, that the house was owned by a Jewish couple. Although I was surprised at the request, I was happy enough to meet them and a few days later an elderly couple – well dressed, but in an old pre-war style – walked into my room and politely introduced themselves as the owners. A few days later, Elsie passed on an invitation from the couple to me for afternoon tea. This was awkward for me for two reasons: firstly, as they were probably in their 70s and I was in my mid-20s the age difference was, for me, a little uncomfortable as I didn't feel I had anything to talk to them about. Secondly, there was the obvious historic legacy of the Holocaust. Being German, I was concerned about the reception I would receive. Eventually they returned to the boarding house once more and invited me in person. This time I did go, and they were very friendly and welcoming. After the pleasantries, they asked me about West Germany and explained that they would very much like to visit but they were afraid to go, given the history of the Holocaust.

Although West Germany had already begun to pay various forms of compensation in 1952,[16] by 1955 there were still no diplomatic relations between Israel and the Federal Republic of Germany. It wasn't until 1960 that Israel's prime minister, David Ben-Gurion, met with the Federal Republic's chancellor, Konrad Adenauer, and stated publicly that the new West Germany was not in any way like the Nazi regime.[17] Still, it took

The boarding house in Norwood, 112 Edward Street, where I was hosted by Arthur and Elsie and which was then owned by Robert and Marcelle Ellis/Elsasser – the parents of Don Dunstan's first wife, Gretel Ellis. (Andrew Gaczol)

until 1965 before full diplomatic relations were established between the two countries.

Despite the official diplomatic situation, I explained to them that they had nothing to fear as nobody would dare do them any harm precisely because of what had occurred under the Nazi regime. The sense of shame was strong, especially amongst the younger generation, and this meant that it was highly unlikely that anything untoward would ever happen to them. Although I advised them to make the trip, I don't know if they did or not. Despite their further invitations, I didn't see them again after Elsie and Arthur returned to Albany. We boarders then had to find alternative accommodation and that effectively cut off my line of communication to the couple.

That was the end of the story. Or so I thought. In 2019, Professor Angela Woollacott published a biography of Don Dunstan, South Australia's Premier during the 1970s.[18] In it she describes his first wife, Gretel Ellis. Professor Woollacott explained that 'Ellis' had, in fact, been Anglicised from the German 'Elsasser' and that Gretel's father had been

The Ellis/Elsasser family. From left to right: Charlotte, Robert, Marcelle and Gretel. (courtesy Dunstan family)

a German Jew and her mother, a Swiss Jew. Both had come to Australia as refugees from the Nazis in the late 1930s and settled in Adelaide.[19] The book further explained that the Ellis family had bought a house in Norwood – 112 Edward Street.

Land Services South Australia confirmed that the owners of the house in 1955 were Robert and Marcelle Ellis/Elsasser and that that the property was sold on 7 November 1955. So the elderly Jewish couple I met that afternoon in 1955 were, in fact, the parents of Don Dunstan's first wife, Gretel Ellis.

We contacted the Dunstan family, who generously confirmed that Robert and Marcelle Ellis had indeed visited Switzerland and Germany in 1957 and that their trip had been both enjoyable and incident free. I'm delighted they took my advice and that all went well.

One final piece of information the Dunstan family provided us was that Don and Gretel held their engagement celebration at the Edward Street house where I had lived.[20] I continue to be amazed at the number of historic coincidences that have touched my life.

My fiancée arrives

Before my fiancée arrived, I thought that I should try to go travelling around Australia. However, as a European, you don't really realise how big Australia is and that travelling from place to place as one would do in Europe is impractical. As an example, one of my German friends, Horst, wanted to go outback and see the Australian bush. To do so, he was advised to go to the north of South Australia and ask the farmers there for work, as they were always looking for people to hire. Eventually, one farmer offered Horst some work in herding sheep. The farmer already had someone working for him and Horst was supposed to relieve him, so he headed out on horseback. After three and half days, he found both the man and the sheep. But after a chat, they both decided that the job wasn't worth the trouble and he headed back to the farmer and resigned, leaving the sheep in the paddock to fend for themselves. Needless to say, the farmer wasn't happy. But Horst's experience showed me just how huge the continent was – that one single sheep farm would need a three and half day ride to cross was, for me, extraordinary. So, I decided to put my travel plans on hold.

By the University of Adelaide footbridge, June 1956. (Otto Gaczol)

In June 1956, my fiancée arrived from West Germany. She had taken the ship the *Fairsea* from Bremerhaven and arrived in Melbourne in mid-June. After I had met Gerhardt on my voyage, his wife and my fiancée had contacted each other in West Germany and arranged to come out together on the same ship. Gerhardt and I then travelled together to Melbourne and picked up both Gerhardt's wife and my fiancée after they had alighted from the ship and made their way through the immigration bureaucracy. We didn't stay in Melbourne long, and returned to Adelaide on the Overland train. My fiancée found accommodation in Barnard Street, North Adelaide. I was, at that time, living in Woodville South and we began the job of organising our wedding. In early July 1956, we were married at the Lutheran Manse in College Park. We then began married life together and lived in Fifth Avenue, Woodville Gardens, from July 1956.

Pastor Zinnbauer

My wife and I had the good fortune to be married by Pastor Alfred Freund-Zinnbauer. Pastor Zinnbauer was born on 26 June 1910 in Vienna to a Jewish father and Catholic mother. Although raised as a Catholic, he trained as a Lutheran pastor and was ordained on 27 July 1936. He was dismissed from his post twelve months later when his Jewish background was discovered.[4]

After failing to obtain a post with the church in Europe or in North America, Pastor Zinnbauer was accepted by the United Evangelical Lutheran Church in Australia. He and his wife arrived in Adelaide on 21 February 1940. Four months later, Pastor Zinnbauer was interned for four years 'chiefly as a precautionary measure'. He was eventually released on 25 February 1944. In April 1945, Zinnbauer was appointed Lutheran city missioner in Adelaide and became a naturalised Australian on 21 February 1946.[5]

When other European refugees and migrants from Europe began arriving in Australia in 1948, Zinnbauer found housing and clothing for them and helped organise schooling for the children. In 1951, he established a hostel at College Park.[6] Pastor Zinnbauer also held church services for migrants and ran Sunday schools for their children. He encouraged them to maintain their language and culture and at the same time urged them to learn English and to become loyal Australians. In 1967, he was appointed MBE; he was also awarded the Officers' Cross of the Order of Merit of the Federal Republic of Germany in 1972 and a Medal of Merit of the Republic of Austria in 1978.[7]

I must admit that I can no longer remember the specific occasion when my wife and I first met Pastor Zinnbauer. We simply met him the way all the migrants of the time did – he was always around the migrant community regardless of where people came from. Apart from our July wedding and December blessing, Pastor Zinnbauer christened both our children when they were born.

Becoming 'New Australians'

It wasn't at all clear that we would remain in Adelaide, or even Australia. Indeed, my wife would have been happy to return to West Germany and at one stage she suggested that we work hard, save money and then go back after two or three years. Although that was an option, I felt I was doing very well here in my new country. In mid-1957, I had found a good job as a tool-setter at Simpson & Sons[25] – an Adelaide company that

My first car, a 1956 Hillman Minx, photographed in 1961. (Otto Gaczol)

built household appliances – and didn't really want to go back. We did, however, agree that if we weren't able to have a family we would return to West Germany.

By 1960, I had bought my first car – a 1956 British Hillman Minx – and together my wife and I built our home in the Adelaide suburb of Klemzig. Although it was only about seven kilometres from the centre of Adelaide, Klemzig was at the time one of the city's outer suburbs and there was a large stock of newly built public housing homes. In the early-1960s, the suburb still had almond groves and other small-scale agriculture in its vicinity and it didn't receive proper street gutters and footpaths until the mid to late 1970s.

Klemzig was one of the places originally settled by the Germans who arrived in 1838. At the time, they established a small village near the River Torrens and named it after their home village back in Germany, which today is now part of Poland and called Klępsk. For many years, the original German cemetery[26] at Klemzig was neglected and overgrown and the neighbourhood children, including my own, used to play there. In 1983, by an Act of Parliament, the site was set aside as a Pioneer Memorial Cemetery[27] and in 1988 it was re-dedicated after its restoration.

In the mid-1960s, our first child was born. Despite having both been in Australia for almost 10 years, we were still German citizens and officially categorised as 'aliens'. With our second child on the way in the late 1960s, we started to give some serious thought as to where we

Outside our Klemzig home with our fellow immigrant friends on the day of my youngest child's christening, late 1960s. Standing in the back with glasses and moustache is Pastor Zinnbauer. We named our house 'Silesia' after our home province in Germany. (Otto Gaczol)

should settle, as we wanted a stable family environment and didn't want to uproot the children.

The Australian government encouraged all new settlers to take out Australian citizenship as it believed that the numbers of settlers taking up citizenship indicated the success of the immigration program. Formal citizenship ceremonies were eventually introduced to highlight its civic importance. As part of official policy, immigrants were called 'New Australians', a term which was intended to be welcoming but also carried with it the expectation that they would adopt Australian ways as quickly as possible. 'Old' Australians were, at the same time, encouraged to be 'good neighbours' and help new arrivals blend in, and in my experience they generally did. The government was concerned that European settlers would form enclaves, decline to contribute to the wider community and possibly undermine Australia's social cohesion. Australians themselves had the option of joining the Good Neighbour Movement, a nationwide organisation founded in 1949. This allowed them to offer their assistance in assimilating the huge numbers of new immigrants into the Australian way of life.

My own experience as a child in Poland very much influenced my decision about whether or not to stay. In the 14 years of my childhood and youth, my family and I moved five times and my mother had found it difficult to find accommodation with two young children. Having now had children of my own, I wanted a settled family environment and didn't want to run the risk of having to regularly relocate as had been my experience as a child in Europe. Also, living in multi-storey apartment houses, as is common in West Germany and throughout continental Europe, can be a very insular and gossipy life where your neighbours know everything about you and privacy is at a premium. All these things were on my mind and in the end I concluded that the lifestyle my wife and I had established in Australia was better than what we could expect back in West Germany.

It wasn't an easy decision to surrender our German citizenship and become Australians but given the family situation and my prosperous employment I felt it was better that we stay in Australia. So, in the second half of 1966, both my wife and I lodged our naturalisation application forms with the Australian Immigration Department and in late December 1966, at the City of Enfield Council Offices, we took the Oath of Affirmation and became Australian citizens.

I was now a 'New Australian' and living in my third country with my third citizenship. And that is my story.

Epilogue

After the late 1960s, my life was essentially settled. My wife and I settled into a routine of domesticity that most people would be familiar with. I continued to work, my wife was a stay-at-home mother (as was generally the case at the time) and our children grew up during the 1970s attending the local primary and high schools. I remained at Simpsons & Sons – later named Simpson Pope – until 1977, when I left and eventually found work at Castalloy Ltd. There I stayed until December 1995 when I finally, and thankfully, retired.

I returned to Europe for the first time in 1974. As we had young children at the time, my wife remained in Australia and I travelled alone. There, I again met my mother and my brother-in-law in Bielefeld. At one stage my brother-in-law suggested returning to West Germany, particularly as the Australian economy had started to slow as a result of the OPEC oil embargo. He was convinced that, being a tradesman, I would have little difficulty finding work. But the reasons I decided to settle in Australia hadn't changed, my children were now in school and ultimately West Germany, too, began to feel the economic bite of the oil embargo. Had I lost my job, I perhaps would have again considered South Africa as I had heard that Germans were popular there, but there was still the racial and political situation to think about. In any case, it didn't matter as I kept my employ and had no need to once again uproot myself.

My wife and I both returned to Europe in 1988 and again in 1996. We visited our home towns in what is now Poland, as well as Bielefeld in the Federal Republic of Germany and, of course, some of the popular tourist destinations as well. In our home towns and in Bielefeld, we reunited with some of the people we both knew before we left for Australia. For my wife, however, the 1988 visit was a year too late as her brother – my brother-in-law – had died the year earlier and, as it turned out, it was also the last time I saw my own mother who died in mid-1990.

Although far away, I watched with interest the changing politics in Eastern Europe. The emergence of *Solidarność* in Poland in the early 1980s, the ascension to power of a reformist Mikhail Gorbachev in the Soviet Union during the mid-1980s were remarkable, but like many others I was still surprised to see the Berlin Wall fall, and how fast the reunification of East and West Germany occurred. Today, both Poland and the reunited Germany have reconciled, have a generally positive relationship and are now partners in the European Union: a supra-national body specifically established so that the conflicts of old cannot re-occur. Australia, too, has changed dramatically since my arrival 60 years ago. Run down and old-fashioned in 1955, Australia has developed into a modern, populous and prosperous nation with a more cosmopolitan and international outlook.

My children are now both adults. I also have two grandchildren and I can look back on what has been a full life. You can see from my recollections that on quite a number of occasions, it was pure serendipity that my life took the direction it did. Surviving a bomb blast during the invasion of Poland, General Patton's unauthorised thrust into Czechoslovakia that allowed me to reach the American lines, and the delayed letter from my friend in Canada that meant I ended up in Australia rather than in North America, all show how much fate can intervene in a person's life.

My life, then, has been shaped by history and with it my family's as well. Had there been no World War II, I would almost certainly not have met my wife and while I might eventually have had children, they would not be the people I know today. Perhaps this is the most important theme of this book: that a person's life is not just about the decisions we make, but also about the uncontrolled circumstances in which we find ourselves.

I hope my story has been of interest to you, and that it helps you reflect on yours.

Bibliography

Government information

'ARCHIVED – Forging Our Legacy: Canadian Citizenship and Immigration, 1900–1977', Canadian Government website: <http://www.cic.gc.ca/english/resources/publications/legacy/chap-5b.asp> retrieved 12 November 2014.

'Bonegilla Migrant Camp', National Film and Sound Archives (Australian Government) website: http://www.nfsa.gov.au/digitallearning/heritage/bonegilla.html> retrieved 20 November 2014.

First Report on the progress and assimilation of migrant children in Australia, Commonwealth Immigration Advisory Council – Special Committee The Progress and Assimilation of Migrant Children in Australia, Canberra, Commonwealth Government Printer, 1960: <www.multiculturalaustralia.edu.au/doc/immadvise_4.pdf> retrieved 23 November 2014.

'Grand Slam Raids', Royal Air Force webpage, <http://www.raf.mod.uk/history/bombercommandgrandslamraids.cfm> retrieved 23 October 2014.

'History of the Bundeswehr', German Ministry of Defence website: <http://www.bmvg.de/portal/a/bmvg/!ut/p/c4/FcwxDoAgDEDRG7W7m6dQ3AAbaIRCkilometresL1xfz15eOFK7GDg-1cxCY80Xje3ASXRwBlH6lF4q61JO78gHvlJp0UGwRSH5fohMc_SgENCdac9w8ftXfP/> retrieved 26 October 2014.

'Immigration chronology: selected events 1840–2008', New Zealand Parliament webpage: <http://www.parliament.nz/en-nz/parl-support/research-papers/00PLSocRP08011/immigration-chronology-selected-events-1840-2008> retrieved 12 November 2014.

'Israel', German Federal Foreign Ministry website: <http://www.auswaertiges-amt.de/EN/Aussenpolitik/Laender/Laenderinfos/01-Nodes/Israel_node.html> retrieved 21 November 2014.

Marsden, S., 'Twentieth Century Heritage Survey, Stage 1: Post Second World War (1946–1959) Overview History', South Australian Department of Environment and Heritage, Adelaide, 2003–04.

'Oral histories on the topic "recession 1961"', Museum of Australian Democracy website: <http://oralhistories.moadoph.gov.au/topics/

recession%201961> retrieved 20 November 2014.

'The changing face of modern Australia – 1950s to 1970s', Australian government website: <http://www.australia.gov.au/about-australia/australian-story/changing-face-of-modern-australia-1950s-to-1970s> retrieved 12 and 20 November 2014.

'The Selective Service System – Immigrants and Dual Nationals', Selective Service System (US Government) website: <https://www.sss.gov/fsaliens.htm> retrieved 11 November 2014.

Books

Bönisch-Brednich, B., 2002, *Keeping a Low Profile: An Oral History of German Immigration to New Zealand*, Victoria University Press, Wellington.

Biddiscombe, P., 2004, *The Last Nazis: SS Werewolf Guerrilla Resistance in Europe 1944–1947*, Tempus Publishing.

—, 1998, *Werwolf!: The History of the National Socialist Guerrilla Movement, 1944–1946*, University of Toronto Press.

Conversino, M.J., 1997, *Fighting with the Soviets: The Failure of Operation Frantic, 1944–1945*, Lawrence, Kansas, University Press of Kansas.

Douglas, R.M., *Orderly and Humane: The expulsion of the Germans after Second World War*, Yale University Press, 2012.

Eisenberg, C.E., 2005, *Drawing the Line: The American Decision to Divide Germany, 1944–1949*, Cambridge University Press.

Henke, Klaus-Dietmar, *Die amerikanische Besetzung Deutschlands*, Munich, Oldenbourg, 1995.

Jupp, J., 1991, *Immigration*, Oxford University Press Australia.

Klusmeyer, D.B. & Papademetriou, D.G., 2009, *Immigration Policy in the Federal Republic of Germany: Negotiating Membership and Remaking the Nation*, Berghahn Books, New York and Oxford.

Konecny, G., Bielitz 1945: *Ein Augenzeugenbericht*, Franken Ferialverbindung, Frankfurt am Main.

McDonough, F., 2001, *Opposition and Resistance in Nazi Germany*, Cambridge University Press, Cambridge.

Miller, D.L., 2006, *Masters of the Air: America's Bomber Boys who fought the War against Nazi Germany*, Simon & Shuster, New York.

Persico, J.E, 1994., *Nuremberg: Infamy on Trial*, Penguin Books, Harmondsworth.

Schult, P., 1978, *Besuche in Sackgassen. Aufzeichnungen eines homosexuellen Anarchisten*, Munich: Trikont Verlag.

Taylor, F., 2004, *Dresden: Tuesday 13 February 1945*, Bloomsbury Publishing, London.

Steber, M. & Gotto, B., eds, 2014, *Visions of Community in Nazi Germany. Social Engineering and Private Lives*, Oxford University Press, Oxford.

Weber, J., 2004, *Germany, 1945–1990: A Parallel History*, CEU Press.

Woollacott, A., *Don Dunstan: The visionary politician who changed Australia*, Allen & Unwin, Sydney, 2019.

Articles

Anh, T. Le, 'Entry into University: Are the children of immigrants disadvantaged?', Business School, The University of Western Australia, Discussion Paper 09.01: <http://www.business.uwa.edu.au/__data/assets/pdf_file/0007/260485/09_01_Le.pdf> retrieved 28 November 2014.

Bignon, V., 'Smoking or Trading?: Cigarette money in post-WW2 Germany', discussion paper, February 2004: <http://economix.fr/docs/54/BignonCigarette.pdf> retrieved 25 October 2014.

Campbell, F.G., 'The Struggle for Upper Silesia, 1919–1922', *The Journal of Modern History*, Vol. 42, No. 3 (Sept. 1970).

Conway, J.S., 'The Twentieth Century Peace Movement in Germany', *Australian Journal of Politics and History*, Vol. 34, No. 4, 1989.

Dickerson, B.J., 'The Liberation of Western Czechoslovakia 1945', Military History Online website: <http://www.militaryhistoryonline.com/wwii/articles/liberation1945.aspx> retrieved 11 October 2014.

Douglas, R.M., 'The Expulsion Of The Germans: The Largest Forced Migration In History', *The Huffington Post*, 25 June 2012, <http://www.huffingtonpost.com/rm-douglas/expulsion-germans-forced-migration_b_1625437.html> retrieved 2 January 2015.

Evans, R., 'The Other Horror', *The New Republic*, 25 June 2012: <http://www.newrepublic.com/book/review/orderly-humane-expulsion-germans-richard-evans> retrieved 10 October 2014.

Gordon, P.H., 'Book Review: 'Joschka Fischer and the Making of the Berlin Republic: An Alternative History of Post-war Germany', *Foreign Affairs*: <http://www.foreignaffairs.com/articles/63131/philip-h-gordon/joschka-fischer-and-the-making-of-the-berlin-republic-an-alterna> retrieved 10 October 2014.

Harris, S., 'The Massacre at Oradour-sur-Glane', Foreign Policy, 5 June 2014: <http://www.foreignpolicy.com/articles/2014/06/05/the_massacre_oradour_sur_glane_wwii_france> retrieved 10 October 2014.

Herbert, U., 'The Army of Millions of the Modern Slave State: Deported, used, forgotten: Who were the forced workers of the Third Reich, and what fate awaited them?' Universitaet Freiburg (published in the *Frankfurter Allgemeine Zeitung*, 16 March 1999; this is an extract from Ulrich Herbert's *Hitler's Foreign Workers: Enforced Foreign Labor in Germany under the Third Reich*, Cambridge University Press 1997: <http://web.archive.org/web/20110604024311/http://www.ess.uwe.ac.uk/genocide/slave_labour13.htm> retrieved 21 October 2014).

Höhn, M., 'Stunde Null der Frauen?: Renegotiating women's place in post-war Germany', in *Stunde Null: The End and the Beginning Fifty Years Ago*, Occasional Paper No. 20, in Giles, G.J., ed., German Historical Institute, Washington DC, 1997.

Karch, B., 'Nationalism on the Margins:

Silesians Between Germany and Poland, 1848–1945: <www.ghi-dc.org/files/publications/bulletin/bu050/039.pdf> retrieved 20 August 2014.

McGhee J.T., 'Waffen SS Part I: Birth of the Elite: A Brief Summary of the Development of the Waffen SS 1939-1940', Military History Online website: <http://www.militaryhistoryonline.com/wwii/articles/waffenss.aspx> retrieved 30 September 2014.

McKenna-Klein, F., 'Germany 1946/47, The Hunger Winter', Bella Online: The Voice of Women website: <http://www.bellaonline.com/articles/art178861.asp> retrieved 27 October 2014.

Michalczyk, A., 'Celebrating the nation: the case of Upper Silesia after the plebiscite in 1921': <eprints.ucl.ac.uk/16348/1/16348.pdf> retrieved 21 August 2014.

Monteath, P., 'Robert Elsasser/Ellis: Refugee and teacher', *Journal of the Historical Society of South Australia*, No. 44, 2016, pp. 51–63.

Motyl, A.J., 'Remembering the Red Army and Rape', 9 May 2014, World Affairs website: <http://www.worldaffairsjournal.org/blog/alexander-j-motyl/remembering-red-army-and-rape> retrieved 2 October 2014.

Rilett, M., 'Zinnbauer, Alfred Freund (1910–1978', Australian Dictionary of Biography webpage, <http://adb.anu.edu.au/biography/zinnbauer-alfred-freund--12095>, accessed 14 January 2018.

Sake, G., 'Should the Allies have bombed Auschwitz?', Academia.edu website: <http://www.academia.edu/4730761/Should_Allies_Have_Bombed_Auschwitz_during_the_Second_World_War> retrieved 24 September 2014.

Sauer, A.E., 'Model Workers or Hardened Nazis?: The Australian Debate about Admitting German Migrants 1950–1952': <http://www.utexas.edu/depts/cas/anzsana/papers/sauer1996.html> retrieved 12 November 2014.

Scheinfeld, J., 'Israeli director dismantles Nazi Jewish soap myth', Jewish Telegraphic Agency website: <http://www.jta.org/2013/06/06/arts-entertainment/israeli-director-dismantles-nazi-jewish-soap-myth> retrieved 13 September 2014.

Service, H., 'Nazi Germany, Communist Poland and the Politics of Ethnicity in Upper Silesia, 1939–1949', University of Cambridge: <http://www.hist.cam.ac.uk/research/research-projects/modern-european/nazi-germany-communist-poland> retrieved 8 March 2013.

Suter, K., 'The Long Boom', Global Directions website: <http://global-directions.com/Articles/Business/TheLongBoom.pdf> retrieved 15 December 2014.

'The Beneš decrees: A spectre over Central Europe', *The Economist*, 15 August 2002: <http://www.economist.com/node/1284252> retrieved 10 October 2014.

Wolf, E.K. & Laumann, A.E., 'The use of blood-type tattoos during the

Cold War', *Journal of the American Academy of Dermatology*, Volume 58, Issue 3, pages 472–476, March 2008: <http://www.jaad.org/article/S0190-9622%2807%2902359-6/fulltext> retrieved 19 October 2014.

'Wood gas vehicles: firewood in the fuel tank' Low-tech Magazine website: <http://www.lowtechmagazine.com/2010/01/wood-gas-cars.html> retrieved 4 October 2014.

Young, G., 'Early German Settlements in South Australia', *Australian Historical Archaeology*, 3, 1985.

Zakrzewski, A., 'Polish Cavalry: A Military Myth Dispelled' Military History Online website: <http://www.militaryhistoryonline.com/wwii/articles/polishcavalry.aspx> retrieved 27 August 2014.

Newspapers and media

Beevor, A., 'They raped every German female from eight to 80', *The Guardian*, 1 May 2002: 'http://www.theguardian.com/books/2002/may/01/news.features11> retrieved 2 October 2014.

Critical Past website: <http://www.criticalpast.com/video/65675068330_armored-columns_vehicles-through-a-town_civilian-smokes-pipe_German-boy-smiles> retrieved 17 October 2014.

Davis, M., BBC website 'Why didn't the Allies bomb Auschwitz?', 23 January 2005: <http://news.bbc.co.uk/2/hi/europe/4175045.stm> retrieved 24 September 2014.

Der Spiegel, 'Der Retter von Dinkelsbühl' ('The Rescuer of Dinkelsbühl'), first published 18 September 1957 (in German): <http://www.spiegel.de/spiegel/print/d-41758550.html> retrieved 17 October 2014.

—, 'Germany's WWII Occupation of Poland: 'When We Finish, Nobody Is Left Alive', 27 May 2011: <http://www.spiegel.de/international/europe/germany-s-wwii-occupation-of-poland-when-we-finish-nobody-is-left-alive-a-759095.html> retrieved 20 September 2014.

—, 'Photo Gallery: Women in the Rubble', 8 October 2010: <http://www.spiegel.de/fotostrecke/photo-gallery-women-in-the-rubble-fotostrecke-56829.html> retrieved on 23 October 2014.

—, 'Wehrmachts-Krankenakte: Dokument nährt die Zweifel an Grass' Angaben', 25 August 2006, (in German): <http://www.spiegel.de/kultur/literatur/wehrmachts-krankenakte-dokument-naehrt-die-zweifel-an-grass-angaben-a-433608.html> retrieved 6 October 2014.

Deutsche Welle, 'The 'du/Sie' dilemma in German': <http://www.dw.de/the-du-sie-dilemma-in-german/a-16494631> retrieved 31 October 2014.

—, 'Remembering Germany's "Rubble Women"': <http://www.dw.de/remembering-germanys-rubble-women/a-1575535-1> retrieved on 23 October 2014.

'Fifty years since the 1961 Bonegilla riot', ABC Goulburn Murray website:

<http://www.abc.net.au/local/stories/2011/07/22/3275388.htm> retrieved 20 November 2014.

'Hitler Youth decorated by Hitler (March 20, 1945)' Youtube: <http://www.youtube.com/watch?v=NtuxrGncxS0> retrieved 3 October 2014.

Mackenzie, J., 'Forgotten German veterans of France's Vietnam war', 2 May 2004; originally published by Reuters: <http://www.theusenetarchive.com/usenet-message-forgotten-german-veterans-of-france-s-vietnam-war-45083381.htm> retrieved 14 November 2014.

'On this day: 1 May 1945: Germany announces Hitler is dead', BBC website: <http://news.bbc.co.uk/onthisday/hi/dates/stories/may/1/newsid_3571000/3571497.stm> retrieved 10 October 2014.

'Sept. 1, 1939 Nazi Germany Invades Poland, Starting World War II' – The Learning Network, New York Times: <http://learning.blogs.nytimes.com/2011/09/01/sept-1-1939-nazi-germany-invades-poland-startingworld-war-ii/?_php=true&_type=blogs&_r=0> retrieved 26 August 2014.

'The Great Patriotic War: 55 years on', BBC, 12 May 2000: <http://news.bbc.co.uk/2/hi/europe/744350.stm> retrieved 10 October 2014.

'Upper Silesia flags up its call for autonomy', in *The Guardian*, 9 April 2011: <http://www.theguardian.com/world/2011/apr/08/upper-silesia-flags-up-independence> retrieved 20 August 2014.

'U.S.A.: German Chancellor Konrad Adenauer meets Israeli Premier David Ben-Gurion in New York', ITN News website: <http://www.itnsource.com/shotlist//RTV/1960/03/15/BGY503240190/> retrieved 21 November 2014.

'Veterans gather to remember Patton's 'greatest, but most terrible sport'', Radio Prague, 8 May 2010: <http://www.radio.cz/en/section/special/veterans-gather-to-remember-pattons-greatest-but-most-terrible-sport> retrieved 6 October 2014.

'World War II's first victim', *The Telegraph* (UK): <http://www.telegraph.co.uk/history/world-war-two/6106566/World-War-IIs-first-victim.html> retrieved 26 August 2014.

Webpages

'A. Simpson & Son', SA Memory: Past and Present for the Future website: <http://www.samemory.sa.gov.au/site/page.cfm?u=1103> retrieved 19 November 2014.

'A Brief History of Upper Lusatia', Oberlausitz website: <http://www.oberlausitz.com/kultur/en/geschichte_oberlausitz.htm> retrieved 6 October 2014.

'Allied occupation and the formation of the two Germanys, 1945–49', Encyclopaedia Britannica Online, <http://www.britannica.com/EBchecked/topic/67354/Bizonia> retrieved 31 October 2014.

'Apartheid and reactions to it', South African History Online website:

<http://www.sahistory.org.za/article/apartheid-and-reactions-it> retrieved 11 November 2014.

'Auschwitz', United States Holocaust Memorial Museum website: <http://www.ushmm.org/wlc/en/article.php?ModuleId=10005189> retrieved 19 September 2014.

'Austria in 1914', Spartacus Educational website: <http://www.spartacus.schoolnet.co.uk/FWWinAustria.htm> retrieved 6 November 2013.

'Bachem Ba 349 B-1 Natter (Viper)', Smithsonian National Air and Space Museum website: <http://airandspace.si.edu/collections/artifact.cfm?object=nasm_A19600313000> retrieved 14 September 2014.

'BAOR Locations', British Army Of the Rhine website: <http://www.baor-locations.org/bielefeldvarious.aspx.html> retrieved 2 January 2015.

'Battle of Dien Bien Phu', Encyclopaedia Britannica Online website: <http://www.britannica.com/EBchecked/topic/162678/Battle-of-Dien-Bien-Phu> retrieved 13 November 2014.

'Bielsko' on the Jewish Virtual Library website: <http://www.jewishvirtuallibrary.org/jsource/judaica/ejud_0002_0003_0_02953.html> retrieved 19 September 2014.

'Bielsko', The Yivo Encyclopaedia of Jews in Eastern Europe website: <http://www.yivoencyclopedia.org/article.aspx/Bielsko> retrieved 21 August 2014.

'Bielsko-Biala' – Official page: <http://www.bielsko.biala.pl/eng> retrieved 21 August 2014.

'Biographies: De-Gi', German Resistance Memorial Centre website: <http://www.gdw-berlin.de/en/recess/biographies/index_of_persons/offset/48/> retrieved 29 October 2014.

'Block 19 today', The Bonegilla Migrant Experience website: http://www.bonegilla.org.au/block19/block19today.asp> retrieved 20 November 2014.

'British Bombing Strategy in World War Two', Siebert, D., BBC History website: <http://www.bbc.co.uk/history/worldwars/wwtwo/area_bombing_01.shtml> retrieved 10 October 2014.

'Cemeteries of the City of Port Adelaide Enfield – Past', City of Port Adelaide and Enfield website: <http://www.portenf.sa.gov.au/page.aspx?u=333> retrieved 21 November 2014.

'Chronology', German-Australia website: <http://www.germanaustralia.com/e/chron/chron7.htm> retrieved 12 November 2014.

'Chronology 1939', Indiana University website: <http://www.indiana.edu/~league/1939.htm> retrieved 25 August 2014.

'Chronology of the Holocaust', United States Holocaust Memorial Museum webpage at: <http://www.ushmm.org/m/pdfs/20000321-holocaust-chronology.pdf> retrieved 19 September 2014.

'Czech-German Declaration', Harold B. Lee Library Brigham Young University website: <http://eudocs.

lib.byu.edu/index.php/Czech-German_Declaration> retrieved 1 October 2014.

'Der Bromberger Blutsonntag' website (in German) at: <http://www.boenend.de/bromberg.htm>, retrieved 12 January 2015.

'Der Reichsarbeitsdienst (RAD)', German Historical Museum website (in German): <https://www.dhm.de/lemo/kapitel/ns-regime/ns-organisationen/arbeitsdienst/> retrieved 4 October 2014.

'Documents of American History II - 1940s: Displaced Persons Act of 1948': <http://tucnak.fsv.cuni.cz/~calda/Documents/1940s/Displaced%20Persons%20Act%20of%201948.html> retrieved 11 November 2014.

'Erwin Rommel', Jewish Virtual Library website: <http://www.jewishvirtuallibrary.org/jsource/biography/Rommel.html> retrieved 15 December 2014.

'Erwin Rommel', Encyclopaedia Britannica Online website: <http://www.britannica.com/EBchecked/topic/508989/Erwin-Rommel#ref210168> retrieved 15 December 2014.

'Forced Labour', Shoah Resource Center, The International School for Holocaust Studies website: <http://www.yadvashem.org/odot_pdf/Microsoft%20Word%20-%206625.pdf> retrieved 21 October 2014.

'Gerda Weissmann Klein' Seminar promotion, University of Wisconsin Eau Claire website: <http://www.uwec.edu/Activities/programs/forum/gerdaWeissmannKlein.htm> retrieved 19 September 2014.

'German administration of occupied Poland', United States Holocaust Memorial Museum website: <http://www.ushmm.org/wlc/en/article.php?ModuleId=10005300> retrieved 20 September 2014.

'German FuG 202 /FuG 220 Lichtenstein airborne radars', Hans H. Jucker: <http://aobauer.home.xs4all.nl/Lichtenstein%20radars.pdf> retrieved 25 September 2014.

'German Fritz X Guided Bomb', US National Air Force Museum website: <http://www.nationalmuseum.af.mil/factsheets/factsheet.asp?id=15564> retrieved 14 September 2014.

'Gestapo', Encyclopaedia Britannica Online, <http://www.britannica.com/EBchecked/topic/232117/Gestapo> retrieved 1 January 2015.

'Gun that shoots around corners', Imperial War Museum website: <http://archive.iwm.org.uk/server/show/ConWebDoc.2482> retrieved 14 September 2014.

'Günter Grass', Encyclopaedia Britannica Online website: <http://www.britannica.com/EBchecked/topic/242123/Gunter-Grass> retrieved 6 October 2014.

'Harry Truman Administration: Directive to Gen. Eisenhower on Military Rule of Germany', Jewish Virtual Museum website: <http://www.jewishvirtuallibrary.org/jsource/ww2/directivegermany.html> retrieved 26 October 2014.

'Historical Overview', Dinkelsbühl website: <http://www.dinkelsbuehl.de/ISY/index.php?PHPSESSID =h89bno95t0jartl9pg8srodt 75&get=488> retrieved 17 October 2014.

'Historie Hrdlovky', Historie Oseka: oficiální stránky mesta website (in Czech): <http://historie.osek.cz/kategorie/historie-okolnich-obci/hrdlovka/historie-hrdlovky> (in Czech) retrieved 1 October 2014.

'History', Bielefeld Tourist Information website: <https://www.bielefeld.de/en/ti1/history/> retrieved 23 October 2014.

'History of Bielsko-Biala', Bielitz-Biala e.V website:<http://www.bielitz-biala.de/index.php?Itemid=33&id=19&option= com_content&task=view> retrieved 3 September 2014.

'Hitler and 'Lebensraum' in the East', Noakes, J., BBC website: <http://www.bbc.co.uk/history/worldwars/wwtwo/hitler_lebensraum_01.shtml> retrieved 11 November 2014.

'Hitler's Boy Soldiers 1939–1945', The History Place website: <http://www.historyplace.com/worldwar2/hitleryouth/hj-boy-soldiers.htm> retrieved 3 October 2014.

'Holocaust Remembrance Day', Council of Europe website: <http://hub.coe.int/27-january-holocaust-remembrance-day> retrieved 29 September 2014.

'Human Fat Was Used to Produce Soap in Gdansk during the War', Auschwitz–Birkenau Memorial and Museum website, 13 October 2006: <http://en.auschwitz.org/m/index.php?option=com_content&task=view&id=55& Itemid=8> retrieved 13 September 2014.

'IG Farben', Encyclopaedia Britannica Online website: <http://www.britannica.com/EBchecked/topic/282192/IG-Farben> retrieved 27 October 2014.

'Indoctrinating Youth', United States Holocaust Memorial Museum website: <http://www.ushmm.org/wlc/en/article.php?ModuleId=10007820> retrieved 14 September 2014.

'Inflation Calculator', Bank of England website: <http://www.bankofengland.co.uk/education/Pages/resources/inflationtools/calculator/flash/default.aspx> retrieved 12 November 2014.

'Johns Perry Limited', Boral website: <http://www.boral.com.au/history/Ch5_10.html> retrieved 20 November 2014.

'Karlovy Vary: Introduction', My Czech Republic website: <http://www.myczechrepublic.com/karlovy-vary/> retrieved 4 October 2014.

'Katyn Memorial Wall' at Electronic Museum website: <http://www.electronicmuseum.ca/Poland-WW2/katyn_memorial_wall/kilometresw_G.html> retrieved 21 September 2014.

'Klemzig Old Lutheran Pioneer Cemetery', Australian Cemeteries website: <http://www.australiancemeteries.com.au/sa/

pt_adel_enfield/klemzigpioneer.htm> retrieved 21 November 2014.

'Klemzig Pioneer Memorial', Monument Australia website: <http://monumentaustralia.org.au/themes/landscape/settlement/display/51029-klemzig-pioneer-memorial> retrieved 21 November 2014.

'Mechanisation', National Army Museum website: <http://www.nam.ac.uk/microsites/war-horse/explore/legacy/mechanisation/> retrieved 27 August 2014.

'MS Seven Seas', SS Maritime website: <http://www.ssmaritime.com/sevenseas.htm> retrieved 12 November 2014.

'Munich', BBC website: <http://www.bbc.co.uk/bitesize/higher/history/roadwar/munich/revision/2/> retrieved 13 January 2015.

'Nazi Labour Camps: Blechhammer (Auschwitz IV)' at the Jewish Virtual Library website: <https://www.jewishvirtuallibrary.org/jsource/Holocaust/Blechhammer.html> retrieved 21 September 2014.

'Nazi persecution of Soviet prisoners-of-war', United States Holocaust Memorial Museum website: <http://www.ushmm.org/wlc/en/article.php?ModuleId=10007178> retrieved 10 October 2014.

'Neuer Lebensraum im Osten Europas', and subsequent webpages at Deutschen Forschungsgmeinshaft website: <http://www.dfg.de/pub/generalplan/planung_1.html> retrieved 11 November 2014.

'Night Vision Devices', DSI: Defence and Security of India, 02 June 2014: <http://defencesecurityindia.com/night-vision-devices/> retrieved 14September 2014.

'One Survivor Remembers', Teaching Tolerance website: <http://www.tolerance.org/kit/one-survivor-remembers> retrieved 19 September 2014.

'Operation Bagration', WW2History.com website: <http://ww2history.com/key_moments/Eastern/Operation_Bagration> retrieved 13 September 2014.

'Poles: Victims of the Nazi era, 1933-1945', Florida Center for Instructional Technology, College of Education, University of South Florida: <http://fcit.usf.edu/Holocaust/people/USHMMPOL.HTM> retrieved 5 September 2014.

'Populate or Perish', Curtin University website: <http://john.curtin.edu.au/1940s/populate/> retrieved 12 November 2014.

'Population estimates for Melbourne, Australia, 1950-2015', Mongabay website: <http://books.mongabay.com/population_estimates/full/Melbourne-Australia.html> retrieved 20 November 2014.

'Postwar Occupation and Division of Germany', German Culture website: <http://www.germanculture.com.ua/library/history/bl_postwar.htm> retrieved 22 October 2014.

'Radio Address by Neville Chamberlain, Prime Minister, September 3, 1939', Yale Law School, The Avalon Project: < http://avalon.

law.yale.edu/wwii/gb3.asp> retrieved 27 August 2014.

'Reichskolonialbund', Die Deutsche Kolonialgesellschaft (DKG) (German Colonial Society) website (in German): <http://www.ub.bildarchiv-dkg.uni-frankfurt.de/Bildprojekt/DKG/DKG.htm#Reichskolonialbund> retrieved 11 November 2014.

'Should the Allies Have Bombed Auschwitz: William J. van den Heuvel vs. Rafael Medoff', History News Network website: <http://historynewsnetwork.org/article/4268> retrieved 24 September 2014.

'Shuttle Raids to Russia', National Museum of the US Air Force website: <http://www.nationalmuseum.af.mil/factsheets/factsheet.asp?fsID=1653> retrieved 22 January 2015.

'Silesia (historical region, Europe)', Encyclopaedia Britannica Online website: <http://www.britannica.com/EBchecked/topic/544097/Silesia> retrieved 20 August 2014.

'South Indian Ocean Tropical Cyclone Season 1954–1955', Australian Severe Weather website: <http://www.australiasevereweather.com/tropical_cyclones/jtwc_1954_1955_south_indian_ocean_tropical_cyclones.htm> retrieved 13 November 2014.

'Sturmabteilung' Encyclopaedia Britannica Online website: <http://www.britannica.com/EBchecked/topic/514736/SA> retrieved 3 October 2014.

'The Beginning of the Final Solution: The Wannsee Conference', Yad Vashem website: <http://www.yadvashem.org/yv/en/holocaust/about/04/wannsee_conference.asp> retrieved 16 December 2014

'The House Of Hanover: Adelaide of Saxe-Meiningen', English Monarchy website: <http://www.englishmonarchs.co.uk/hanover_17.html> retrieved 20 November 2014.

'The Institute for Research of Expelled Germans' (Institut für Vertriebenenforschung) website: <http://expelledgermans.org/> retrieved 10 October 2014.

'The Nazi Party: Hitler Youth', Jewish Virtual Library website: <http://www.jewishvirtuallibrary.org/jsource/Holocaust/hitleryouth.html> retrieved 14 September 2014.

'The need for German rearmament', Centre Virtuel de la Connaissance sur l'Europe (CVCE), 14 May 2013: <http://www.cvce.eu/obj/the_need_for_german_rearmament-en-be64df30-92d8-4e3c-bd97-d870e3d6a121.html> retrieved 26 October 2014.

'The Sixty-First Anniversary of the Liberation of Auschwitz', 27 January 2006, Auschwitz-Birkenau Museum website: <http://en.auschwitz.org/m/index.php?option=com_content&task=view&id=121&Itemid=8> retrieved 29 September 2014.

'The Thousand Bomber Raid', History Learning Site website: <http://www.historylearningsite.co.uk/thousand_bomber_raid.htm> retrieved 1 January 2015.

'Vessel Type EC2: The Liberty

Ship', Skylighters website: <http://www.skylighters.org/troopships/libertyships.html> retrieved 11 November 2014.

'Waikerie', Explore Australia website: <http://www.exploreaustralia.net.au/South-Australia/Murray/Waikerie> retrieved 20 November 2014.

'World War II: Closing the Falaise Pocket', originally published by World War II magazine. Published Online: June 12, 2006: <http://www.historynet.com/world-war-ii-closing-the-falaise-pocket.htm> retrieved 26 November 2014.

'World War II: The Soviet advance to the Oder, January – February 1945', Encyclopaedia Britannica Online website: <http://www.britannica.com/EBchecked/topic/648813/World-War-II/53598/The-Soviet-advance-to-the-Oder-January-February-1945> retrieved 27 September 2014.

'398th Bomb Group Combat Formations', Blackwell, W., 398th Bomb Group Memorial Association website: <http://www.398th.org/Research/8th_AF_Formations_Description.html> retrieved 12 October 2014.

'4lb Incendiary Bomb', Boyd, D., World War 2 Equipment website: <http://www.wwiiequipment.com/index.php?option=com_content&view=article&id=114:4lb-incendiary-bomb&catid=43:bombs&Itemid=60> retrieved 13 September 2014.

Television broadcasts

Damals in der DDR, episode one, 'Aufbruch in Trümmern' ('Dawn amongst the Ruins'), MDR Broadcasting Germany, 2004.

The World at War, BBC documentary series, episode 21, 'Nemesis', 1974.

Who do you think you are?, Special Broadcasting Service Australian television: <http://www.sbs.com.au/shows/whodoyouthinkyouare/episodes/detail/episode/4694/season/5> retrieved 10 October 2014.

Correspondence

Email correspondence with James Mayfield, Director of the Institute for Research of Expelled Germans, 18 October 2014.

Notes

One

1. 'Austria in 1914', Spartacus Educational website.
2. Campbell, F.G., 'The Struggle for Upper Silesia, 1919–1922', p. 361.
3. 'Silesia (historical region, Europe)', Encyclopaedia Britannica Online website.
4. Ibid.
5. Karch, B., 'Nationalism on the Margins: Silesians Between Germany and Poland, 1848–1945', p. 46.
6. Ibid., pp. 50–52.
7. Michalczyk, A., 'Celebrating the nation: the case of Upper Silesia after the plebiscite in 1921'.
8. See 'Upper Silesia flags up its call for autonomy', in *The Guardian*, 9 April 2011.
9. Karch, B., 'Nationalism on the Margins: Silesians Between Germany and Poland, 1848–1945, pp. 50–52. James Mayfield, Director of the Institute for Research of Expelled Germans, observed that 'the main reasons behind the Silesians' exemption was primarily because most 'Silesians' (as was classified in 1945) were seen by the new Polish government and the communists as a regional variation of Polish culture. As a result, Warsaw was suspicious of them for their regionalism and potential ambiguity but did not brand them as 'mixed' or German… Most authentic Germans were expelled, as well as most Silesian Poles who claimed to be German under occupation. They ceased to be Polish essentially. Another key cause is the fact that occupied Germany already had 3–5 million refugees from Poland and could not cope with the remaining Silesian German expellees. Moscow, Warsaw, London, and Washington agreed to hold them back in Poland either under surveillance or in concentration camps… Many were later deported.' Email from James Mayfield.
10. 'Bielsko-Biala' – official page: <http://www.bielsko.biala.pl/eng> retrieved 21 August 2014.
11. 'Bielsko', The Yivo Encyclopaedia of Jews in Eastern Europe website.
12. Ibid.
13. Ibid.
14. The agreement ceded the Sudetenland to Nazi Germany, and also resulted in Czechoslovakia's further dismemberment when Poland annexed Teschen and Hungary annexed Ruthenia. See 'Munich', BBC website.
15. 'Chronology 1939', Indiana University.

Two

1. 'Sept. 1, 1939 Nazi Germany Invades Poland, Starting World War II' – The Learning Network, New York Times.
2. There is a nice summary of the event in 'World War II's first victim', *The Telegraph* (UK).
3. There are few English language sources for this event. In 1996, a joint Polish-German documentary was produced. See the 'Der Bromberger Blutsonntag' website (in German). The program summary states, 'To this day there are two fundamentally different versions of this story. In Polish schoolbooks, it is written that an uprising by patriotic citizens was crushed by Nazi agents. The then German residents say that Polish commandos dragged innocent Germans from their homes and murdered them. The Nazis then used the "Bromberg Blood Sunday" to justify the invasion of Poland and their own retaliation massacres. Later, Poland used the events as the reason behind the German expulsions.' (Author's translation)
4. 'Gestapo' is an acronym of *Geheime Staatspolizei* (Secret State Police). It was the political police of the Nazi regime and eliminated opposition to the Nazis within Germany and its occupied territories. See 'Gestapo', Encyclopaedia Britannica Online.
5. 'Radio Address by Neville Chamberlain, Prime Minister, September 3, 1939', Yale Law School, The Avalon Project.
6. 'Although Germany's "Blitzkrieg" strategy focused on the use of tanks with motorised infantry and air support, the German army still relied heavily upon horses for supply transport and pulling artillery…' 'Mechanisation', National Army Museum website.
7. Zakrzewski, A., 'Polish Cavalry: A Military Myth Dispelled' Military History Online website.
8. This is confirmed by a history of Bielsko-Biala currently available on the internet: 'Am 3. September 1939 ziehen österreichische Verbände der Deutschen Wehrmacht kampflos in Bielitz ein und werden von der deutschen Bevölkerung begeistert begrüßt. (On 3 September 1939 Austrian regiments of the German Wehrmacht arrive in Bielsko without resistance and are enthusiastically welcomed by the German population.)' 'History of Bielsko-Biala', Bielitz-Biala e.V website. The troops were apparently from the Hoch und Deutschmeister Division.
9. A summary is provided at 'German administration of occupied Poland', United States Holocaust Memorial Museum website.
10. Klusmeyer, D.B. & Papademetriou, D.G., 2009, pp. 68–69.
11. Steber M.& Gotto, B., pp. 135–136.
12. Service, H., 'Nazi Germany, Communist Poland and the Politics of Ethnicity in Upper Silesia, 1939–1949', University of Cambridge.
13. Klusmeyer, D.B., &. Papademetriou, D.G., pp. 68–69.

14. A full description including technical details can be found at 'German FuG 202 /FuG 220 Lichtenstein airborne radars', Hans H. Jucker4.

15. The various sources of information on the Hitler Youth list different dates when membership became compulsory. The reference to 1939 is 'Indoctrinating Youth', United States Holocaust Memorial Museum website, while the 1941 date is from the Jewish Virtual Library, 'The Nazi Party: Hitler Youth', Jewish Virtual Library website.

16. See Conversino, M.J., 1997. See also, Miller, D.L., 2006, p. 323, which talks about how the USAAF 15th Air Force were bombing targets in Upper Silesia near Auschwitz. There is also a short summary at 'Shuttle Raids to Russia', National Museum of the US Air Force website.

17. The Combat Box Formation was made up of a number of basic airplane relationships. From the smallest to the largest, these formations were element formation, three planes; squadron formation, four elements, 12 planes; group formation, three squadrons, 36 planes; and wing formation, three groups, 108 planes. See '398th Bomb Group Combat Formations', Blackwell, W., 398th Bomb Group Memorial Association website.

18. This may have been the attack of 7 August 1944 when the USAAF attacked the refinery at Trzebina, which was 55 kilometres from Bielsko-Biala. See 'Operation FRANTIC', Wikipedia. Or perhaps it could have been the attack of 9 September 1944, when USAAF bombers destroyed large parts of the plants of the Oberschlesische Hydrierwerke AG served by the notorious Blechhammer labour camp and of the oil refinery in Trzebinia. See 'Nazi Labour Camps: Blechhammer (Auschwitz IV)' at the Jewish Virtual Library website.

19. It is very likely that these were the Royal Air Force's 4lb (1.8kg) incendiary bombs. These are described further at '4lb Incendiary Bomb', Boyd, D., World War 2 Equipment website.

20. 'The Thousand Bomber Raid', History Learning Site website. The website provides a figure of 600 acres of the city destroyed, which converts to approximately 2.42 square kilometres.

21. 'Gun that shoots around corners', Imperial War Museum website.

22. Known as the 'Fritz X', these bombs were a 1,500kg armour-piercing bomb. See 'German Fritz X Guided Bomb', US National Air Force Museum website.

23. The Smithsonian National Air and Space Museum has a good summary 'Bachem Ba 349 B-1 Natter (Viper)', Smithsonian National Air and Space Museum website.

24. The German company AEG manufactured them. They were the 'Solution A – Sperber FG 1250' with Panther tanks and the 'Vampir' man portable system for infantry. See 'Night Vision Devices', DSI: Defence and Security of India, 02 June 2014.

25. This observation is made in an overall sense – proportionally Croatia and Belarus lost larger shares of their populations during the Nazi occupation. Email of 18 October 2014 from James Mayfield, Director of the Institute for Research of Expelled Germans.

26. A summary can be found at: 'Poles: Victims of the Nazi era, 1933–1945', Florida Center for Instructional Technology, College of Education, University of South Florida. Also, the German magazine Der Spiegel, 'Germany's WWII Occupation of Poland: 'When We Finish, Nobody Is Left Alive', 27 May 2011.

27. See Persico, J.E., p. 250 and pp. 358–359.

28. See the 'Katyn Memorial Wall' at Electronic Museum website, which lists the victims of the killings, including Adolf Jozef Gaczol.

29. A full summary can be found at 'Chronology of the Holocaust', United States Holocaust Memorial Museum webpage.

30. From 'Bielsko' on the Jewish Virtual Library website.

31. 'Gerda Weissmann Klein', seminar promotion, University of Wisconsin Eau Claire website.

32. "One Survivor Remembers', Teaching Tolerance website.

33. 'Auschwitz', United States Holocaust Memorial Museum website.

34. 'The Beginning of the Final Solution: The Wannsee Conference', Yad Vashem website.

35. 'Human Fat Was Used to Produce Soap in Gdansk during the War', Auschwitz-Birkenau Memorial and Museum website, 13 October 2006.

36. Scheinfeld, J., 'Israeli director dismantles Nazi Jewish soap myth', Jewish Telegraphic Agency website.

37. The debate about whether the Allies should have bombed Auschwitz, and the reasons why they didn't, is a passionate and controversial one. There are a number of books and articles on the topic. There is one of many summaries on the BBC website: Davis, M., BBC website 'Why didn't the Allies bomb Auschwitz?', 23 January 2005.

38. Sake, G., 'Should the Allies have bombed Auschwitz?', Academia.edu website.

39. See 'Should the Allies Have Bombed Auschwitz: William J. van den Heuvel vs. Rafael Medoff', History News Network website.

40. Klusmeyer, D.B. & Papademetriou, D.G., p. 69.

41. 'Operation Bagration', WW2History.com website.

42. 'World War II: Closing the Falaise Pocket', originally published by *World War II* magazine; published online 12 June 2006.

Three

1. 'World War II: The Soviet advance to the Oder, January–February 1945', Encyclopaedia Britannica Online website.

2. The war on the eastern front had

little mercy. Under Nazi race 'theory', the people of Poland, Ukraine and Russia were considered Slavic *Untermenschen* (subhumans) and treated accordingly. Of all the Red Army's soldiers captured as prisoners of war, 3.3 million (about 57% of those taken prisoner) were dead by the end of the war. See 'Nazi persecution of Soviet prisoners-of-war', United States Holocaust Memorial Museum website.

3. Motyl, A. J., 'Remembering the Red Army and Rape', 9 May 2014, World Affairs website.

4. Beevor, A., 'They raped every German female from eight to 80', *The Guardian*, 1 May 2002. Beevor has, however, received criticism of his statistical analysis and the two million figure he calculated remains controversial.

5. For example, of the out of the 91,000 German soldiers captured after the battle of Stalingrad, only 6,000 survived the prison camps and returned home – most of them dying through disease and neglect. See 'The Great Patriotic War: 55 years on', BBC, 12 May 2000.

6. The German television series 'Damals in der DDR' ('Back then in East Germany') documented this aspect of the Soviet occupation of eastern Germany. They gave the example of Gerhard Fischer who, as a 15-year-old, was arrested in 1945 and then continuously interrogated until he signed a confession saying he was a Werewolf underground resistance fighter. He was then imprisoned and eventually sent to Siberia only being released after four years. See episode one '*Aufbruch in Trümmern*' ('Dawn amongst the Ruins'), MDR Broadcasting, Germany, 2004.

7. 'The Sixty-First Anniversary of the Liberation of Auschwitz', 27 January 2006, Auschwitz-Birkenau Museum website.

8. For example, 'Holocaust Remembrance Day', Council of Europe website.

9. An account was written in German on the experience in Bielsko-Biala. See Konecny, G..

10. The 1974 BBC documentary series *The World at War* shows some footage of Allied fighters even attacking a lone man on a horse and cart. See episode 21 'Nemesis'.

11. The village no longer exists. When it was discovered that the village sat atop a coal seam, the decision was made in the late 1960s/early 1970s to resettle its occupants to the nearby town of Osek and demolish the town to mine the coal. Some photos can be found at: 'Historie Hrdlovky', Historie Oseka: oficiální stránky mesta website (in Czech).

12. 'Sturmabteilung' Encyclopaedia Britannica Online website.

13. The dying days of the Nazi regime saw many young teenage boys thrown into battle. There is a short film of Hitler decorating some of his so-called 'boy soldiers' during March 1945 in the gardens of the Berlin Chancellery. See 'Hitler's Boy Soldiers 1939–1945', The History Place website, and 'Hitler Youth decorated by Hitler (March 20, 1945)', Youtube.

14. Still debated today, the destruction of Dresden – and indeed other German cities in the last six months of the war – was questionable given the superior military situation that the Allies were enjoying and the indiscriminate nature of the bombing. By March 1945, even PM Winston Churchill expressed his disquiet and penned a memorandum to the RAF Bomber Command leadership stating: 'It seems to me that the moment has come when the question of bombing of German cities simply for the sake of increasing the terror, though under other pretexts, should be reviewed… The destruction of Dresden remains a serious query against the conduct of Allied bombing.' See 'British Bombing Strategy in World War Two', Siebert, D., BBC History website. The most authoritative source on the city and its destruction is Taylor, Frederick, 2004.

15. McGhee J.T., 'Waffen SS Part I: Birth of the Elite: A Brief Summary of the Development of the Waffen SS 1939–1940', Military History Online website.

16. 'On June 10, 1944, four days after the Allied landing at Normandy, a unit of the Waffen-SS…descended on the village and killed 642 men, women, and children. It was one of the largest mass murders of French civilians during the German occupation, and an act of retribution against the townspeople for their perceived assistance to the French Resistance and the invading American forces.' Harris, S., 'The Massacre at Oradour-sur-Glane', *Foreign Policy*, 5 June 2014.

17. See Biddiscombe, P., 2004, and Biddiscombe, P., 1998.

18. See 'On this day: 1 May 1945: Germany announces Hitler is dead', BBC website.

19. Karlovy Vary (Karlsbad) is a famous spa town which was founded in 1350 by the Czech King and Holy Roman Emperor Charles IV. The town has had many famous visitors over the years including Ludwig van Beethoven, Wolfgang Amadeus Mozart and Franz Kafka. See the 'Karlovy Vary: Introduction', My Czech Republic website.

20. See 'Der Reichsarbeitsdienst (RAD)', German Historical Museum website (in German).

21. There is a useful description of such cars at 'Wood-gas vehicles: firewood in the fuel tank', Low-tech Magazine website.

22. An historic summary of the region can be found at: 'A Brief History of Upper Lusatia', Oberlausitz website.

23. For a detailed discussion see Dickerson, B.J., 'The Liberation of Western Czechoslovakia 1945', Military History Online website.

24. There is reference to our camp, and the unauthorised advance of General Patton into Czechoslovakia in this article 'Veterans gather to remember Patton's "greatest, but most terrible sport"', Radio Prague, 8 May 2010. A former US serviceman remembered, 'We went to Marienbad for a short time after that, and there was a huge displaced persons camp there at the airport. I can't estimate

how many were there, probably several thousand. And all we were doing there was guarding them so they wouldn't walk away, but they didn't want to go because they were getting food and bathing facilities and I guess getting a paper so they could leave.'

25. Der Speigel, ‚Wehrmachts-Krankenakte: Dokument nährt die Zweifel an Grass' Angaben', 25 August 2006 (in German). This article details Grass's whereabouts during that period through the examination of documents detailing his medical treatment and transfers.

26. 'Günter Grass', Encyclopaedia Britannica Online website.

27. Douglas, R.M., 'The Expulsion Of The Germans: The Largest Forced Migration In History', *The Huffington Post*, 25 June 2012.

28. There was a change of government in the UK following the July 1945 general election; Atlee, leader of the Labour Party, replaced Churchill as prime minister during the period of the conference.

29. An academic institute, Institut für Vertriebenenforschung (The Institute for Research of Expelled Germans), has been founded to help document this history. Some of this summary has been taken from their website: <http://expelledgermans.org/> retrieved 10 October 2014.

30. Douglas, R.M., 2012, p. 94. This publication is considered a balanced, fair and well-researched study. Richard Evans, Regius Professor of History and President of Wolfson College at Cambridge University, provided a summary and review at 'The Other Horror', *The New Republic*, 25 June 2012.

31. A summary of the continued impact of these decrees can be found in an article 'The Beneš decrees: A spectre over Central Europe', The Economist, 15 August 2002. It is worth noting that the governments of the Czech Republic and the Federal Republic of Germany have signed an international agreement recognising these events. Through this document, both governments expressed regret and the desire to move forward. See 'Czech-German Declaration', Harold B. Lee Library Brigham Young University website.

32. The Institute for Research of Expelled Germans (Institut für Vertriebenenforschung) webpage.

33. Gordon, P.H., 'Book Review: 'Joschka Fischer and the Making of the Berlin Republic: An Alternative History of Post-war Germany', *Foreign Affairs*.

34. Who Do You Think You Are?, Special Broadcasting Service Australian television.

Four

1. A good summary can be found at 'Postwar Occupation and Division of Germany', German Culture website.

2. See 'Harry Truman Administration: Directive to Gen. Eisenhower on Military Rule of Germany', Jewish Virtual Museum website.

3. A summary can be found at 'IG Farben', Encyclopaedia Britannica Online website.

4. Eisenberg, C.E., p. 148.

5. 'In September 1944, 5.5 million foreign workers and two million prisoners of war were working in Germany; 38 per cent of those were Soviet and 20 per cent were Polish. By the end of that year, another 1.5 million forced labourers had been recruited... Eastern European forced labourers were treated much worse than those from Western Europe... although Western European workers had better living and working conditions, they also complained that they were treated like slaves.' See 'Forced Labour', Shoah Resource Center, The International School for Holocaust Studies website. See also: Herbert, U., 'The Army of Millions of the Modern Slave State: Deported, used, forgotten: Who were the forced workers of the Third Reich, and what fate awaited them?' Universitaet Freiburg (published in the Frankfurter Allgemeine Zeitung, 16 March 1999). This is an extract from Herbert's *Hitler's Foreign Workers: Enforced Foreign Labor in Germany under the Third Reich*, Cambridge University Press, 1997.

6. Despite the initial intention to defend the city until the end, an agreement was reached between the city authorities and the German armed forces that Dinkelsbühl was to be surrendered without a fight. As a result, the city was occupied by US troops unopposed on 20 April 1945. See 'Der Spiegel, 'Der Retter von Dinkelsbühl' ('The Rescuer of Dinkelsbühl'), first published 18 September 1957 (in German). Footage of the US troops moving through Dinkelsbühl can be seen at the 'Critical Past' website:.

7. 'Historical Overview', Dinkelsbühl website.

8. Members of the SS had their blood group tattooed on their skin so that medical treatment could be quickly administered in case of being wounded: 'Each member of the Waffen-SS had a blood-type tattoo under the left axilla on the inner arm or chest wall.' See Wolf, E.K. & Laumann, A.E., 'The use of blood-type tattoos during the Cold War.', *Journal of the American Academy of Dermatology*, Volume 58, Issue 3, pp. 472–476, March 2008.

9. The *Edelweißpiraten* were a group of non-conformists during the Third Reich who rejected political assimilation into the Hitler Youth and other Nazi organisations. After war they for the most part, similarly rejected the youth groups set up by the Allies. See McDonough, F., 2001, pp. 15–20. As references also see Schult, P., p. 46, and Henke, Klaus-Dietmar, pp. 198–200.

10. See 'Grand Slam Raids', Royal Air Force webpage.

11. A number of photos of the ruined city and the destroyed viaduct can be found at 'BAOR Locations', British Army Of the Rhine website.

12. 'History', Bielefeld Tourist Information website.

13. 'In 1945, there were approximately seven million more women in Germany than men. More than three million German soldiers were killed in the war and a further seven million were still prisoners-of-war.' Höhn, M., 'Stunde Null der Frauen?: Renegotiating women's place in post-war Germany', in *Stunde Null: The End and the Beginning Fifty Years Ago*, Occasional Paper No. 20, in Giles, G.J. (ed.), German Historical Institute, Washington DC, 1997, p. 76.

14. Deutsche Welle, 'Remembering Germany's 'Rubble Women', and *Der Spiegel*, 'Photo Gallery: Women in the Rubble', 8 October 2010.

15. McKenna-Klein, F., 'Germany 1946/47, The Hunger Winter', Bella Online: The Voice of Women website.

16. Frings had also spoken out against Nazi persecution during the period 1942–44. This earned him the attention of the Gestapo. See 'Biographies: De-Gi', German Resistance Memorial Centre website.

17. McKenna-Klein, F., op. cit.

18. Ibid.

19. In German, the word *Du* is an informal method of address normally used amongst friends and family while the formal *Sie* is used with acquaintances and work colleagues. For further explanation, see *Deutsche Welle*, 'The 'du/Sie' dilemma in German'.

20. Bignon, V., 'Smoking or Trading?: Cigarette money in post-WW2 Germany', discussion paper, February 2004.

21. 'Allied occupation and the formation of the two Germanys, 1945–49', Encyclopaedia Britannica Online.

22. Weber, J., pp. 31–32.

23. 'The need for German rearmament', Centre Virtuel de la Connaissance sur l'Europe (CVCE), 14 May 2013.

24. Conway, J.S., 'The Twentieth Century Peace Movement in Germany', *Australian Journal of Politics and History*, Vol. 34, No. 4, 1989, pp 79–81.

25. 'History of the Bundeswehr', German Ministry of Defence website.

26. The SPD has a long history going back to 1875, and it was outlawed soon after the Nazis came to power in 1933. Reformed after the war, it was the only surviving party from the pre-war period with an unblemished record of opposition to Hitler and the Nazis. See 'Social Democratic Party of Germany (SPD)', Encyclopaedia Britannica Online.

Five

1. 'Reichskolonialbund', Die Deutsche Kolonialgesellschaft (DKG) (German Colonial Society) website (in German).

2. A good summary of the concept can be found on the BBC website: 'Hitler and Lebensraum 'in the East', Noakes, J., BBC website. Another website (in German) explains in detail the development of Generalplan Ost. See 'Neuer Lebensraum im Osten Europas', and subsequent webpages

at Deutschen Forschungsgmeinshaft website.

3. 'Apartheid and reactions to it', South African History Online website.

4. 'Liberty ships' were mass produced ships designed and built as troop transport and supply ships during World War II. A summary can be found at: 'Vessel Type EC2: The Liberty Ship', Skylighters website.

5. 'Documents of American History II – 1940s: Displaced Persons Act of 1948'.

6. 'U.S. non-citizens and dual nationals are required by law to register with the Selective Service System. Most are also liable for induction into the U.S. Armed Forces if there is a draft.' See 'The Selective Service System – Immigrants and Dual Nationals', Selective Service System (US Government) website.

7. The Canadian government had, in 1950, liberalised its immigration policies. Although it retained the preference for British, Irish, French, and American immigrants; and widened the admissible classes of European immigrants to include any healthy applicant of good character who had skills needed in Canada and who could easily integrate into Canadian society. The Canadian government also took German immigrants off the enemy–alien list (Italian immigrants had been removed from the list in 1947). As a result, Germans joined the increasing numbers of Italians in applying for admission to Canada.

See 'ARCHIVED – Forging Our Legacy: Canadian Citizenship and Immigration, 1900–1977', Canadian Government website.

8. 'Populate or Perish', Curtin University website. See also Jupp, J., 1991. chapter 6, 'Populate or Perish: Post-War Immigration'.

9. 'The changing face of modern Australia – 1950s to 1970s', Australian government website.

10. 'Chronology', German-Australia website.

11. Sauer, A.E., 'Model Workers or Hardened Nazis?: The Australian Debate about Admitting German Migrants 1950–1952'.

12. In 1947, the New Zealand Government introduced an assisted-passage scheme for British and Irish citizens. British ex-servicemen received the most favourable treatment. In 1950 the policy was amended to extend the categories of British citizens eligible for assistance. It also provided for pacts with other countries for the migration of single men and women aged 20 to 35 years. See 'Immigration chronology: selected events 1840–2008', New Zealand Parliament webpage. It was only in 1950 that New Zealand began to consider male German immigrants and then only on a limited basis. Fears of Germans with a Nazi history was strong and a deep-seated fear of German immigration was apparent during 1950–1954. It was only when New Zealand joined the Intergovernmental Committee for

European Migration in 1956, that greater access to New Zealand by potential German male immigrants was considered. See Bönisch-Brednich, B., pp. 66–69.

13. See a summary of the ship and its history at: 'MS Seven Seas', SS Maritime website.

14. One Australian pound was 0.8 pound Sterling. Using the Bank of 'Inflation Calculator', Bank of England website, 0.8 of one pound Sterling in 1955 was the equivalent of 18.3 pounds Sterling in 2015 – roughly the equivalent of 30 to 45 Australian dollars today, depending on the exchange rate.

15. There were a number of cyclones in the Indian Ocean during the period the MS Seven Seas sailed. So, it is hard to pinpoint which one was encountered. See: 'South Indian Ocean Tropical Cyclone Season 1954–1955', Australian Severe Weather website.

16. As it turns out, there were quite a number of Germans serving in the French Foreign Legion at that time. See Mackenzie, J., 'Forgotten German veterans of France's Vietnam war', 2 May 2004: 'An estimated 35,000 Germans served during the eight-year conflict that ended 50 years ago this week when a disastrous defeat at the battle of Dien Bien Phu on May 7, 1954 brought about the fall of France's colonial empire in Indochina. Many were combat veterans from the army or SS members recruited straight from prisoner of war camps after Germany's defeat.' Originally published by Reuters:.

17. See 'Battle of Dien Bien Phu', Encyclopaedia Britannica Online website.

Six

1. 'Population estimates for Melbourne, Australia, 1950–2015', Mongabay website.

2. See 'Block 19 today', The Bonegilla Migrant Experience website.

3. 'Bonegilla Migrant Camp', National Film and Sound Archives (Australian Government) website.

4. 'Oral histories on the topic "recession 1961"', Museum of Australian Democracy website.

5. 'Fifty years since the 1961 Bonegilla riot', ABC Goulburn Murray website.

6. 'Waikerie', Explore Australia website.

7. Marsden, S., 'Twentieth Century Heritage Survey, Stage 1: Post Second World War (1946–1959) Overview History', South Australian Department of Environment and Heritage, Adelaide, 2003–04, p. 12.

8. 'The House Of Hanover: Adelaide of Saxe-Meiningen', English Monarchy website.

9. See Young, G., 'Early German Settlements in South Australia', *Australian Historical Archaeology*, 3, 1985, pp. 43–55.

10. Perry Engineering started in 1897 when Samuel Perry, a blacksmith from Shropshire, came to Adelaide from Great Britain and started a foundry and forge. The company survived both the

Great Depression and World War II and in 1947, it became a public company. In 1956, the South Australian economy was buoyant, and Perry Engineering started to make mechanical presses for the car industry. General Motors, Ford and Chrysler had all decided to build large steel press shops there. During the next eight years, the company manufactured about four hundred mechanical presses for automotive and general industry. In 1965 Sir Thomas Playford, who had been the Liberal Premier of South Australia for twenty-nine years, was voted out of office. At the same time, the expansion of the car industry tapered off, BHP completed its steelworks at Whyalla and the Torrens Island power station had been completed. Ten years of boom in South Australia came to an end. In 1966 Perry Engineering merged with the Melbourne-based engineering and lift company, Johns & Waygood, which had been operating since the 1860s. The company was called Johns & Waygood Perry Engineering and did not change its name to Johns Perry until 1976. See 'Johns Perry Limited', Boral website.

11. The 'long boom' began at the end of World War II in 1945 and it ended in 1973. It was the longest period of consistent economic growth in world history. It was a time of low unemployment, generally low inflation greater choice of consumer goods and a general sense of economic optimism about the future. See Suter, K., 'The Long Boom', Global Directions website.

12 Australian businessman Arvi Parvo, who also emigrated from Europe, later commented, 'I arrived in South Australia as an immigrant from Europe in November 1949 and spent almost seven years there… In spite of the substantial inflow of immigrants there was an acute shortage of people to do all the work that was available. Living standards were improving, not spectacularly but steadily, as they were throughout Australia. To someone like myself, the contrast with the war-torn Europe I had left behind could not have been greater.' in Marsden, S., 'Twentieth Century Heritage Survey, Stage 1: Post Second World War (1946–1959) Overview History', South Australian Department of Environment and Heritage, Adelaide, 2003–04, p. 12.

13. 'South Australia's post-war boom derived from manufacturing that expanded with state government encouragement and federal government protection. From World War II the Commonwealth subscribed to Keynesian economic theory and used import quotas and tariffs to protect local manufacturing industries. Foreign and domestic investment was concentrated in industries such as clothing, consumer goods and cars, catering for the Australian market. By the mid-1950s, the expansion of manufacturing, together with immigration bringing in both workers and consumers, triggered an economic boom. The biggest gains were made in car and appliance manufacturing and their feeder industries, which grew with the boom in consumer

spending after the war.' Marsden, S., op. cit., p. 26.

14. The Afrika Korps or German Africa Corps was the German expeditionary force in North Africa under the command of LTGEN Erwin Rommel during the Second World War. The Afrika Korps fought in Africa from March 1941 until its surrender in May 1943. See 'Erwin Rommel', Jewish Virtual Library website, and 'Erwin Rommel', Encyclopaedia Britannica Online website.

15. A number of studies have shown that migrant children do very well when compared to Australian born children. For example: 'However, children born overseas with migrant parents (first-generation Australians) have higher tertiary entrance scores than native-born children.' in Anh T. Le, 'Entry into University: Are the children of immigrants disadvantaged? Business School, The University of Western Australia, Discussion Paper 09.01, p. 1. See also First Report on the progress and assimilation of migrant children in Australia, Commonwealth Immigration Advisory Council – Special Committee The Progress and Assimilation of Migrant Children in Australia, Canberra, Commonwealth Government Printer, 1960. 'Our investigations show that most young migrants – about 97 per cent – settle down well to life in Australia; as a group, they are above-average in scholarship…'.

16. 'Since the conclusion of the 1952 Luxembourg Agreement (payment of some EUR 1.53 billion), compensation has been a major political issue in relations between Israel and the Federal Republic of Germany.' 'Israel', German Federal Foreign Ministry website.

17. 'I was glad to meet Chancellor Adenauer. My people never forgot the past but we remember the past not in order to brood upon it but in order that it shall never recur. I said in the Knessett, (the Israeli Parliament), last summer that the Germany of today is not the Germany of yesterday, and having met the Chancellor, I am sure that judgment was correct. I wish the Chancellor every success in his efforts to guide Germany in its path of democracy and international co-operation.' Prime Minister David Ben-Gurion cited from 'U.S.A.: German Chancellor Konrad Adenauer meets Israeli Premier David Ben-Gurion in New York', ITN News website.

18. Woollacott, A., *Don Dunstan: The visionary politician who changed Australia*, Allen & Unwin, Sydney, 2019.

19. A more complete discussion of the Ellis/Elsasser family can be found at: Monteath, P., 'Robert Elsasser/Ellis: Refugee and teacher', *Journal of the Historical Society of South Australia*, No. 44, 2016, pp. 51–63.

20. Email from Ms Bronwen Dohnt, 24 March 2020.

21. Rilett, M., Zinnbauer, Alfred Freund (1910–1978), Australian Dictionary of Biography webpage, <http://adb.anu.edu.au/biography/zinnbauer-alfred-freund--12095>, accessed 14 January 2018.

22. Ibid.
23. Ibid.
24. Ibid.
25. Alfred Simpson and his family arrived in South Australia in 1849. Simpson manufactured many products for agricultural uses and, as agricultural industries became more established in South Australia, so his business, known as the 'Colonial Tinware Manufactory', expanded. In the 1860s, Simpson began manufacturing safes, which became well-known for their ability to resist attempts to blow them open with dynamite. In the late 1880s A. Simpson & Son manufactured munitions and mines, when a war between the British Empire and Russia loomed. By 1891, A. Simpson & Son had the largest metal manufacturing plant in Australia. During the First World War, Simpsons returned to the manufacture of munitions and in the 1920s the company expanded further. A new factory was opened at Dudley Park in the 1940s and the company began the manufacture of whitegoods. In 1963 A. Simpson & Son merged with Pope Industries to form Simpson Pope Holdings. The Simpson brand, now owned by Electrolux, continues to produce a variety of household appliances. 'A. Simpson & Son', SA Memory: Past and Present for the Future website.

26. 'Klemzig Old Lutheran Pioneer Cemetery', Australian Cemeteries website; and Klemzig Pioneer Memorial', Monument Australia website.

27. 'Cemeteries of the City of Port Adelaide Enfield – Past', City of Port Adelaide and Enfield website.

Andrew Gaczol was born in Adelaide, South Australia. He graduated with a Bachelor of Arts from the University of Adelaide in 1994, was awarded a PhD from the Flinders University of South Australia in 2000 and an MPhil from the University of Cambridge in 2009.

He is currently employed as a Senior Research Officer with the House of Representatives, Parliament House, Canberra.

One Life, Three Countries is his first book.

www.ingramcontent.com/pod-product-compliance
Lightning Source LLC
Chambersburg PA
CBHW070908080526
44589CB00013B/1226